FRENCH BISTRO COOKING

FRENCH BISTRO COOKING

Patricia Bourne

First published in 1984 by Octopus Books Limited
59 Grosvenor Street, London W1

© 1984 Hennerwood Publications Limited

ISBN 0 86273 108 9

Produced by Mandarin Publishers Ltd
22a Westlands Road,
Quarry Bay,
Hong Kong

Printed in Hong Kong

CONTENTS

INTRODUCTION

French Bistro Cooking recreates the atmosphere of those unpretentious little restaurants in provincial France where the menu is chalked on a board, the tablecloths are checked gingham, the wine is vin ordinaire – and the food is excellent.

In general, bistro cooking is fairly straightforward – there are no over-fussy or elaborate dishes, and presentation is kept simple. The essence of it is good food well cooked.

Each chapter contains both traditional and new recipes. In 'Soups and Hors d'Oeuvre' there are old favourites such as French onion soup and Pâté de campagne – items any self-respecting bistro owner could do standing on his head – as well as more unusual dishes such as Crêpes stuffed with seafood.

'Sautés and Grills' covers those dishes which take 30 minutes or less to cook: Beef stroganoff, Filet de porc normande, Steak au poivre and so on.

'Main Meals' covers the slow-cooking dishes such as casseroles and roasts. Boeuf à la bourguignonne and Bourride are traditional, but try the more unusual Sauté de porc coriandre (Pork stew with coriander) or Venaison au cassis (Venison with blackcurrants).

In France, great care is taken over the buying and preparation of vegetables. It is quite usual for vegetables, or a salad, to be served separately after the main course, rather than all together in the meat-and-two-veg style of English cooking. The dishes given here can all be served on their own – some substantial enough to make a main course.

The last chapter covers both hot puddings, such as Apple and almond tart and Baked stuffed peaches, and cold sweets, such as rich Suprême au chocolat or the easily prepared Raspberries with figs.

Cooking with Wine
French food and wine are complementary, not only at the table but in the kitchen as well. Meat is often marinaded overnight in wine before it is cooked: the acid in the wine helps to tenderize the fibres of the meat. Red wine is mainly used for this, principally because it is the red meats and game that need tenderizing. The mixture of herbs, spices and vegetables included in the marinade all give extra flavour to the meat.

Which wine should be used for cooking? The simple test is: Can you drink it? It does not have to be expensive, though bear in mind that a rough red wine is unlikely to improve the flavour of anything.

Serving Wine
When choosing a wine to accompany your food, there are particular combinations which go well together and some which should be avoided.

Generally, you can serve the same wine with the hors d'oeuvre and the main course, unless, for instance, you are serving fish for the first course and serving red wine with the main course. Avoid serving wine with salads or hors d'oeuvre with a sharp dressing, as these ruin the flavour of the wine. Egg dishes also tend to give wine a peculiar flavour.

White wine goes well with fish. Try a Muscadet or one of the crisp Loire wines, especially with shellfish.

The usual rule with meat is to serve white wine with white meats (pork, veal, chicken, turkey and rabbit) and red wine with red meats and game (beef, lamb, pheasant, venison, etc.). However, a good Bordeaux (claret) is delightful with roast turkey or chicken and red wine can also be served with pork.

With beef or lamb nothing could be better than a fine claret or Burgundy, while rosé goes well with pork, veal, cold chicken and salads.

To serve with dessert, choose Sauternes, or a nutty Montbazillac, which is delicious with strawberries. Chocolate desserts are best served on their own, as they tend to mask the full flavour of the wine.

Serve white and rosé wines chilled. Red wines are served at room temperature, except for young Beaujolais which can be served chilled, and remember that red wines should be opened to breathe an hour or two before they are drunk.

Cheeses
The excellence of French cheeses is renowned, so it is no wonder that the French make such a display of their cheese boards. The cheese course is an important part of the meal, following after the main course or vegetables and before the dessert. It is eaten with a knife and fork, on its own or with crusty French bread.

It is estimated that there are over 400 cheeses made in France, every region having its own speciality.

From the French Alps comes Gruyère, the cheese most usually used in cooking. It is a very large cheese, easily identified by the holes which form during manufacture. It has a firm, slightly rubbery texture, with a sweet, nutty or fruity flavour. In France, Gruyère is the generic name for all cheeses of this type. Emmental has a slightly stronger flavour and larger holes.

Brie and Camembert are the two cheeses most easily available in this country. They are rich cream cheeses, easily identified by their downy white rind. They have a chalky consistency which changes to a soft cream as they ripen. Brie is the mildest, Carré de l'Est has a similar flavour to Camembert, but is softer in texture. Similar cheeses include Pont l'Évêque and Livarot, as well as the stronger tasting Munster. They are most usually considered to be eating cheeses but Camembert is sometimes used in cooking, particularly in Normandy where it is often used in a filling for pancakes.

Goat's cheeses are made all over France, and they come in many shapes: Chèvre Long or Ste Maure, a long cylindrical cheese, and Valençay with its flattened pyramid shape being the best known. They have a chalky texture with a sharp acidic flavour. Usually eaten at the end of a meal, they can also be used in a refreshing hors d'oeuvre or salad.

The most expensive French cheese – considered by some to be the finest in the world – is Roquefort, a blue cheese made from ewe's milk. It has a butter-like texture and a smooth tangy flavour. At its best, it should have an even marbling of greenish veins. Eat it on its own or use it for salads, canapés and sandwiches. Added to soup, it gives a flavour all of its own.

Fromage blanc is often served as a dessert. This is a soft cheese, the consistency of whipped cream, which is eaten with sugar and sometimes cream as well. Cremets d'Angers are moulded cream cheeses of this type. Fromage blanc is delicious served with fresh fruit. It can also be used as a salad dressing.

Petit-Suisse are tiny cream cheeses with a higher fat content. They are also eaten with sugar or fruit.

When choosing cheeses for your cheese board, pick out three or four contrasting ones. If they need to ripen, it is a good idea to buy them a day or two in advance. If necessary, leave them in a warm room so that they are at their best when you eat them. Take all cheeses out of the refrigerator at least an hour before they are needed, so that the flavour has a chance to develop.

With good food, good wine and good cheese, you will be able to recreate the atmosphere of France in your own home.

Bon Appétit!

LEFT FROM THE TOP: Pont l'Évêque, Chèvre, Petit-Suisse, Roquefort, Munster. RIGHT FROM THE TOP: Emmental, Brie, Camembert, Gruyère

SOUPS & HORS D'OEUVRE

PÂTÉ DE CAMPAGNE
Country Pâté

Serves 8-12
50 g (2 oz) butter, plus extra for greasing
2 onions, peeled and finely chopped
4-5 garlic cloves, peeled and crushed
450 g (1 lb) pig's liver, cut into large dice
275 g (10 oz) streaky bacon rashers, rinded
450 g (1 lb) lean pork, minced or chopped
2 tablespoons chopped fresh parsley
½ teaspoon dried sage
¼ teaspoon ground mace
2 good pinches nutmeg
¼ teaspoon salt
freshly ground black pepper
2 egg whites
2 tablespoons brandy
4 bay leaves

Preparation time: 30 minutes, plus cooling
Cooking time: 1½ hours
Oven: 190°C, 375°F, Gas Mark 5

1. Melt the butter in a frying pan, add the onions and garlic and cook gently for a few minutes until tender. Transfer to a large bowl.
2. Add the liver to the pan and fry until lightly browned and just set. Mince or coarsely chop in a food processor.
3. Chop 225 g (8 oz) of the streaky bacon. Add to the bowl with the liver, pork, parsley, sage, mace, nutmeg, salt, pepper, egg whites and brandy. Mix well.
4. Place in a lightly greased 450 g (1 lb) terrine or tin. Cover with the remaining 50 g (2 oz) streaky bacon rashers. Place 2 bay leaves on top.
5. Put in a bain-marie or roasting tin of hot water. Place in a preheated oven and cook for about 1½ hours or until the juices run clear and the pâté has shrunk slightly from the sides of the tin.
6. When cooked, cool for 30 minutes, then cover with a piece of greaseproof paper or foil and weight lightly. Leave until completely cold and set. Do not pour off any fat or liquid as this will be absorbed back into the pâté. [F]
7. Replace the bay leaves with 2 fresh ones and leave for about 36 hours in a refrigerator.
[F] Over-wrap after step 6 and freeze for up to 1 month. Thaw overnight in the refrigerator.

SOUPE À L'OIGNON
Brown Onion Soup

Serves 5
50 g (2 oz) butter
750 g (1½ lb) onions, peeled and thinly sliced
2 teaspoons sugar
2 teaspoons plain flour
1 litre (1¾ pints) beef stock
salt
freshly ground black pepper
½ French loaf, sliced
50 g (2 oz) Gruyère cheese, grated

Preparation time: 15 minutes
Cooking time: 50 minutes-1 hour

1. Melt the butter in a pan, add the onions and sugar. Lower the heat and cook the onions slowly for 20-30 minutes, until they are an even chestnut brown. Take care to cook them slowly, so that they brown evenly and to a good colour without burning.
2. Add the flour and cook for about 5 minutes, stirring well. Add the stock, salt and pepper. Bring to the boil and simmer for 15-20 minutes.
3. Meanwhile, place the slices of French bread under a preheated grill and toast on one side. Cover the other side with the grated cheese and toast until golden brown.
4. Taste and adjust the seasoning, then pour the soup into a hot tureen. Place a piece of toast in each serving dish and pour the soup over.

Variation:
Prepare the soup up to the end of step 2. Pour it into a wide tureen, or individual soup bowls, and stir in 50 g (2 oz) grated Gruyère or Parmesan cheese. Toast the French bread slices on both sides and float on top of the soup. Sprinkle another 50 g (2 oz) grated Gruyère or Parmesan cheese on top and sprinkle with 1 tablespoon melted butter. Bake for 20 minutes in an oven preheated to 160°C, 325°F, Gas Mark 3, then place under a preheated grill for 1-2 minutes to brown the top lightly.

LEFT TO RIGHT: Pâté de campagne; Soupe à l'oignon

FROMAGE DE CHÈVRE ET TOMATES
Goat's Cheese and Tomato Hors d'Oeuvre

225 g (8 oz) Ste Maure or other goat's cheese
¼ cucumber, thinly sliced
3-4 large continental tomatoes, sliced
Dressing:
4 tablespoons good flavoured oil, preferably olive oil
2 tablespoons wine vinegar
good pinch of dry mustard
salt
freshly ground black pepper
1-2 teaspoons finely chopped fresh parsley or chives

Preparation time: 10 minutes

1. Cut the cheese into 5 mm (¼ inch) slices. On individual plates, arrange the slices of cheese over-lapping in a semi-circle round the top half of each plate.
2. Arrange the cucumber on top of the cheese.
3. Overlap the tomato slices around the bottom half of each plate.
4. To make the dressing, mix or shake the oil, vinegar, mustard, salt and pepper together.
5. Spoon a little dressing over the tomatoes and sprinkle with the chopped parsley or chives. Extra vinaigrette can be served separately if desired.

Variation:
Fresh basil can be used instead of parsley or chives.

GOUGÈRE AU FROMAGE
Cheese Ring

75 g (3 oz) Gruyère cheese
50 g (2 oz) ham, chopped
salt
freshly ground black pepper
65 g (2½ oz) Choux pastry
1 egg, beaten
1 tablespoon chopped blanched almonds

Preparation time: 10 minutes
Cooking time: 30-35 minutes
Oven: 220°C, 425°F, Gas Mark 7;
then: 190°C, 375°F, Gas Mark 5

1. Cut 50 g (2 oz) of the cheese into very small dice and thinly slice the remainder. Mix the diced cheese, ham, salt and pepper into the pastry.
2. Put the mixture into a piping bag fitted with a 1 cm (½ inch) plain nozzle.
3. Lightly grease a baking sheet and mark it with a 15 cm (6 inch) saucepan lid. Using this mark as a guide, pipe the choux pastry into a ring.
4. Brush the pastry with beaten egg and sprinkle it with the slices of cheese and chopped almonds.
5. Place in a preheated oven for 10 minutes, then reduce the oven temperature and cook for a further 25-30 minutes. Place on a hot dish and serve at once.

Variation:
Make a thick béchamel sauce with 40 g (1½ oz) butter, 40 g (1½ oz) flour and 300 ml (½ pint) milk. Omit the ham from the Gougère. Instead, mix 100 g (4 oz) ham and/or 50-100 g (2-4 oz) sliced mushrooms into the sauce. Pipe out 12-16 choux balls onto a lightly greased baking sheet. Continue with steps 4 and 5 above, and fill with the sauce.

CHOUX PASTRY

150 ml (¼ pint) water
50 g (2 oz) butter
65 g (2½ oz) strong plain flour, sifted
2 eggs, beaten

Preparation time: 20 minutes
Cooking time: as given in recipes
Oven: 220°C, 425°F, Gas Mark 7;
then: 190°C, 375°F, Gas Mark 5

1. Put the water and butter in a pan over a low heat until the butter has melted, then increase the heat until the water boils and rises in the pan.
2. Immediately add the flour and beat well over the heat until the mixture leaves the side of the pan and forms a ball. Remove from the heat and leave to cool for a few minutes.
3. Beat in the eggs, a little at a time. Beat each addition of egg in well until the mixture regains its original stiff consistency. An electric mixer can be used at this stage but if an aluminium pan is used, it is essential to transfer the mixture to a bowl before adding the eggs because the action of the beaters on the saucepan could discolour the mixture.
4. Use as required. If baked, the choux pastry should be cooked in a preheated hot oven for the first 10 minutes so that it rises rapidly. The oven tempera-ture is then reduced for the remainder of the time.

TOP TO BOTTOM: Potage au Roquefort; Fromage de Chèvre et tomates

POTAGE AU ROQUEFORT
Roquefort Soup

Serves 4-6

40 g (1½ oz) butter
2 carrots, peeled and cut into small dice
2 onions, peeled and thinly sliced
1 stick celery, cut into small dice
1 leek, trimmed and thinly sliced
40 g (1½ oz) plain flour
1 litre (1¾ pints) chicken stock
150 ml (¼ pint) milk
½ teaspoon salt
white pepper
2 tablespoons double or whipping cream
50-75 g (2-3 oz) Roquefort or other blue cheese

Preparation time: 20 minutes
Cooking time: 30 minutes

1. Melt the butter in a pan, add the carrots, onions, celery and leek and cook gently, stirring continuously, for 7-10 minutes. Do not allow them to brown.

2. Add the flour and cook for 1-2 minutes, then pour on the stock. Bring to the boil, stirring well. Add the milk, salt and pepper, bring to the boil again and cook gently until the vegetables are tender. A F

3. Blend the cream and cheese together in a bowl.

4. Pour on some of the hot soup and mix well together. Return to the pan and stir or whisk over a gentle heat until all the cheese has melted. Heat through without boiling. Serve hot.

A Can be prepared the day before and stored in a refrigerator when cold.

F Defrost overnight in a cool place or in the refrigerator.

PISSALADIÈRE À LA NIÇOISE
French Pizza

Serves 4-6
175 g (6 oz) strong plain flour
¼ teaspoon salt
15 g (½ oz) fresh yeast or 1½ teaspoons dried yeast and 1
    teaspoon caster sugar
6-8 tablespoons tepid water
oil, for brushing
Filling:
2-3 tablespoons oil
450 g (1 lb) medium onions, peeled and thinly sliced
2 garlic cloves, peeled and crushed
1 × 400 g (14 oz) can tomatoes, with juice
salt
freshly ground black pepper
6-8 anchovy fillets, cut into strips
12 black olives

**Preparation time: 30-40 minutes, plus rising and
proving**
Cooking time: 35-40 minutes
Oven: 200°C, 400°F, Gas Mark 6;
then: 180°C, 350°F, Gas Mark 4

This pizza could be used as a lunch or light supper
dish accompanied by a salad.

1. Sift the flour and salt into a large bowl and make a
well in the centre. Dissolve the yeast, and the sugar if
used, in 2 tablespoons of the water. Pour into the
flour with the remaining water. Mix to a smooth
dough, adding a little more water if necessary.
Knead well.
2. Place in a lightly oiled bowl, cover, and leave in a
warm place for about 1 hour or until doubled in size.
3. Meanwhile, to make the filling, heat the oil in a
pan, add the onions and garlic and cook gently until
soft but not coloured. Add the tomatoes and their
juice, salt and pepper and cook until most of the
moisture has evaporated. Leave to cool.
4. When the dough is ready, turn it out on to a
lightly floured board, knead well, then form it into a
20 cm (8 inch) round on a greased baking sheet.
5. Brush with oil and cover with the onion and
tomato mixture. Arrange the anchovies in a lattice
on top and garnish with the olives.
6. Leave to prove in a warm place for 15 minutes.
7. Place in a preheated oven and cook for 15
minutes, then reduce the oven temperature and cook
for a further 20-25 minutes.

LEFT TO RIGHT: Pissaladière a la Niçoise; Artichauts au gratin

ARTICHAUTS AU GRATIN
Baked Artichokes

4 globe artichokes
2 tablespoons lemon juice
65 g (2½ oz) butter
100 g (4 oz) bacon, rinded and finely diced
2 medium onions, peeled and finely chopped
175 g (6 oz) mushrooms, coarsely chopped
25 g (1 oz) plus 2 teaspoons plain flour
2 tablespoons sherry or Madeira
4 tablespoons chicken stock
salt
freshly ground black pepper
pinch of nutmeg
1 tablespoon chopped fresh parsley
300 ml (½ pint) milk
100 g (4 oz) Gruyère cheese, grated

Preparation time: 40 minutes
Cooking time: 50 minutes-1 hour
Oven: 200°C, 400°F, Gas Mark 6

Use young fresh artichokes for this dish, as old or stale ones are tough to cut. This dish could be used for a light lunch or supper dish.

1. Cut off the artichoke stalks close to the base.
2. Using a pair of scissors or a sharp knife, cut through the leaves about 2.5 cm (1 inch) from the base. Using a teaspoon or ball cutter, carefully remove the feathery choke from the centre; then with a small sharp knife or pair of scissors, pare away the tops of the leaves until only the succulent bases of the leaves are left joined to the base, forming a deep cup. Brush with lemon juice.
3. Place the artichokes in a pan of boiling salted water with the remaining lemon juice and cook for about 30 minutes until tender.
4. Meanwhile, melt 40 g (1½ oz) of butter in a pan, add the bacon and fry until golden brown; remove from the pan with a slotted spoon and drain on paper towels. Add the onions to the pan and cook until soft. Add the mushrooms and cook until the onions and mushrooms are tender and the mixture is dry.
5. Return the bacon to the pan. Add 2 teaspoons of the flour and cook for 1-2 minutes, then pour on the sherry or Madeira and the stock. Bring to the boil, stirring well, and cook for 1-2 minutes. Add the salt, pepper, nutmeg and parsley.
6. In another pan, melt the remaining butter, add the remaining flour and cook for 2-3 minutes, stirring. Add the milk and bring to the boil, stirring all the time, and cook for 2-3 minutes. Add half the cheese.
7. When the artichokes are cooked, drain them well and place in a buttered ovenproof dish. Fill the centre of each with some of the mushroom mixture and coat the top with the sauce. Sprinkle the remainder of the cheese over the top. A
8. Place in a preheated oven and cook for 10-15 minutes until brown. Serve hot.
A Can be made earlier in the day and reheated for 15-20 minutes.

Cutting off the stalk

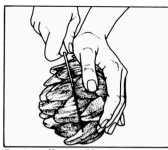
Cutting off tops of leaves

Spooning out the choke

Trimming leaves

FRITOTS AUX MOULES
Mussel Fritters

1 kg (2 lb) mussels
1 small onion, peeled and finely chopped
1 garlic clove, peeled and crushed
4 tablespoons white wine or water
oil, for deep frying
Batter:
50 g (2 oz) plain flour
pinch of salt
65 ml (2½ fl oz) tepid water
2 teaspoons oil
1 egg white

Preparation time: 15-20 minutes, plus resting
Cooking time: 20-30 minutes

1. Check the mussels and discard any which are open or damaged. With a sharp knife, remove the barnacles and beards, and scrub well in several changes of water.
2. Place the mussels in a pan with the onion, garlic and wine or water. Cover and cook over a high heat for 5-6 minutes, shaking the pan vigorously once or twice. By this time all the mussels should have opened.
3. If any are still closed, return to the heat for a few more minutes. Discard any which remain closed. Allow to cool, then remove them from the shells. [A]
4. To make a fritter batter, sift the flour and salt into a bowl. Make a well in the centre and pour in the water and oil. Beat in the flour from the sides until the mixture is smooth. Leave to rest for about 30 minutes.
5. Heat the oil to 190°C (375°F) or until a cube of bread browns in 30 seconds.
6. While it is heating, whisk the egg white stiffly, then gently fold it into the batter mixture.
7. Dip each mussel into the batter and drop into the hot oil. Take care not to overfill the pan. When crisp and golden brown, remove from the pan, drain on paper towels and keep hot until all the mussels have been fried.
8. Serve hot with Sauce tartare (page 15).
[A] The mussels can be prepared and taken from the shells early in the day and kept refrigerated until required.

COURGETTES AUX CREVETTES
Courgettes with Prawns

4 medium courgettes, trimmed
salt
25 g (1 oz) butter
1 medium onion, peeled and finely chopped
2 tomatoes, skinned, seeded and chopped
75 g (3 oz) peeled prawns, coarsely chopped
1-2 tablespoons fresh white breadcrumbs
freshly ground black pepper
3-4 drops Tabasco sauce
1-2 teaspoons lemon juice
1-2 tablespoons grated Parmesan cheese

Preparation time: 20 minutes
Cooking time: 25-30 minutes
Oven: 190°C, 375°F, Gas Mark 5

Choose good, thick courgettes, about 12 cm (4½ inches) long.

1. Place the courgettes in a pan of boiling, salted water and cook for about 5 minutes. Drain and refresh under cold running water.
2. Meanwhile, melt the butter in a pan, add the onion and cook until soft but not coloured.
3. Cut the courgettes in half lengthways and carefully scoop out some of the flesh with a small teaspoon or a ball cutter.
4. Chop the flesh and mix with the onion, tomatoes and prawns. Add sufficient breadcrumbs to give a reasonably dry mixture and add salt, pepper, Tabasco sauce and lemon juice to taste.
5. Pile the mixture into the courgette shells and sprinkle with the Parmesan cheese. Place in a buttered ovenproof dish. [A]
6. Place in a preheated oven and cook for about 20 minutes until the cheese has lightly browned.
[A] Can be made earlier in the day and kept in the refrigerator until required.

LEFT TO RIGHT: Fritots aux moules, Sauce tartare;
Courgettes aux crevettes

SAUCE TARTARE

300 ml (½ pint) Mayonnaise (page 16)
salt
white pepper
2 teaspoons finely chopped capers
2 teaspoons finely chopped gherkins
2 teaspoons finely chopped chives
2 teaspoons finely chopped fresh tarragon

Preparation time: 10 minutes

If fresh tarragon is not available use chopped parsley or fennel.

1. Make the mayonnaise, adding a little salt and pepper.
2. Add the capers, gherkins, chives and tarragon. Taste and adjust the seasoning.
3. Cover and keep 7-10 days in the refrigerator or in a cool place until required.

BEIGNETS AUX CHAMPIGNONS
Mushroom Fritters

225 g (8 oz) flat cap mushrooms, trimmed
3-4 tablespoons seasoned flour
1-2 eggs, beaten
75 g (3 oz) white breadcrumbs, sieved
oil, for deep frying

Preparation time: 10 minutes
Cooking time: 20-25 minutes

1. Dip each mushroom into the seasoned flour, then into the egg and coat with the breadcrumbs. [A]
2. Heat the oil to 190°C (375°F) or until a cube of bread browns in 30 seconds. Fry the mushrooms, a few at a time, until they are golden brown. Drain on paper towels.
3. Serve hot with Aïoli (Garlic mayonnaise) (page 38) or Sauce tartare.
[A] Prepare earlier in the day and keep refrigerated until required.

TOMATES AU THON
Tomatoes with Tuna Fish

4 large tomatoes
1 × 225 g (8 oz) can tuna fish, drained
150 ml (¼ pint) Mayonnaise
salt
freshly ground black pepper
1 teaspoon finely chopped fresh parsley

Preparation time: 15 minutes

This is another dish which could be used for lunch or supper, served with a salad.

1. Place the tomatoes stalk side down and, with a sharp knife, cut 4 or 5 slices down through each one, leaving it joined at the base, so that it opens out like the leaves of a book.
2. With a fork, blend the tuna fish well with 1 tablespoon of the mayonnaise and the salt and pepper. It can be left coarsely mixed, or blended to a smooth paste according to personal preference.
3. Spoon the fish mixture into each slit in the tomatoes.
4. If the mayonnaise is very stiff, mix it with a little hot water to give a firm coating consistency. If liked, coat the top of each tomato with a spoonful of the remaining mayonnaise and sprinkle with a little chopped parsley.

Variation:
Salmon or sardines can be used instead of tuna fish.

MAYONNAISE

Makes 300 ml (½ pint)
1-2 egg yolks or 1 whole egg
½ teaspoon dry mustard
good pinch of caster sugar
¼ teaspoon salt
white pepper
300 ml (½ pint) oil, preferably olive oil
2-3 tablespoons wine vinegar

**Preparation time: 15 minutes by hand;
about 5 minutes with a food processor or liquidizer**

COCKTAIL DE PAMPLEMOUSSE
Grapefruit Cocktail

2 large grapefruit
225 g (8 oz) peeled prawns
75 g (3 oz) sweetcorn, cooked or canned
1 tablespoon whisky
little caster sugar (optional)
pinch of cayenne pepper
150 ml (¼ pint) Mayonnaise
1 teaspoon finely chopped fresh parsley
4 large lettuce leaves

Preparation time: 20-25 minutes

1. Cut the grapefruit in half and carefully remove the segments with a grapefruit knife. Discard the tough skin and cores and reserve any juice.
2. With a small pair of scissors, cut the edge of the grapefruit into a zig-zag pattern (called vandyking).
3. Mix the prawns with the grapefruit segments and juice in a bowl. Add the sweetcorn and whisky and, if the grapefruit are very sharp, add just a little sugar, taking care not to make them sweet. Add the cayenne pepper and toss the mixture well together.
4. Pile the prawn mixture into the grapefruit skins.
5. Place the Mayonnaise in a piping bag fitted with a small star nozzle. Pipe a border of Mayonnaise just inside the decorated edges of the skins. Pipe a swirl of mayonnaise in the centre of each one and sprinkle with chopped parsley.
6. Place each grapefruit half on a large lettuce leaf on a serving dish. Keep chilled until served.

1. Place the egg yolks in a bowl and add the mustard, sugar, salt and white pepper. Blend well together.
2. Drip in the oil slowly from the end of a teaspoon, beating all the time.
3. When the mixture starts to thicken, add 1 tablespoon of the wine vinegar and continue to add the oil a little more quickly. When all the oil has been incorporated, add sufficient vinegar to taste.
4. If using a food processor or liquidizer, place the whole egg, mustard, sugar, salt and white pepper in the container. Switch to fast speed and slowly pour in the oil in a thin stream. Add 1 tablespoon vinegar to the liquidizer when the sauce starts to thicken. Taste and adjust the seasoning.
5. Store, covered, for up to 1 week in the refrigerator.

LEFT TO RIGHT: Avocats et crabe; Tomates au thon

AVOCATS ET CRABE
Avocados and Crab

2 medium to large ripe avocados
1 tablespoon lemon juice
225 g (8 oz) white crab meat, flaked
150 ml (¼ pint) Mayonnaise (page 16)
2-3 teaspoons tomato purée or ketchup
2-3 drops Tabasco sauce
1 teaspoon finely chopped fresh parsley or chives

Preparation time: 15 minutes

1. Cut the avocados in half and remove the stone. With a teaspoon, carefully remove the flesh from the skins and cut into dice.
2. Mix the flesh with the lemon juice to prevent discoloration and replace in the skins, leaving a small well in the centre.
3. Pile the crab meat in the avocado centres, heaping it up as much as possible.
4. Blend the Mayonnaise with sufficient tomato purée or ketchup to colour and flavour, and add the Tabasco sauce to taste.
5. Coat the crab with the sauce and sprinkle with a little chopped parsley or chives.

TERRINE DE CHAMPIGNONS
Mushroom Pâté

Serves 6
65 g (2½ oz) butter
1 onion, peeled and finely chopped
2 garlic cloves, peeled and crushed
450 g (1 lb) mushrooms, chopped
50 g (2 oz) fresh white breadcrumbs
2 eggs, separated
salt
freshly ground black pepper
pinch of nutmeg
To finish:
Sauce hollandaise
1 lemon, thinly sliced
sprigs of parsley

**Preparation time: 30 minutes
Cooking time: 50 minutes-1 hour
Oven: 180°C, 350°F, Gas Mark 4**

1. Butter the inside of a 450 g (1 lb) loaf tin with about 15 g (½ oz) of the butter. Line the base with greaseproof paper and butter again.
2. Melt the remaining butter in a pan, add the onion and garlic and cook until soft but not coloured. Add the mushrooms and cook until the mixture is dry.
3. Purée the mixture in a food processor or liquidizer. (If a liquidizer is used, it may be necessary to use the egg yolks at this stage.)
4. Place the purée in a large bowl and add the breadcrumbs and egg yolks, mixing well. Add the salt, pepper and nutmeg.
5. Beat the egg whites until they are very stiff and carefully fold into the mixture. Pour into the prepared tin.
6. Put the loaf tin in a bain-marie or roasting tin of hot water. Place in a preheated oven and cook for 30-40 minutes until the pâté is firm and sponge-like. [A]
7. Turn out on to a hot serving dish and coat carefully with a little of the sauce. Serve the rest of the sauce separately.
8. Arrange half slices of lemon down the length of the terrine with small sprigs of parsley tucked under each.
[A] The terrine can be prepared and cooked the day before and reheated in a bain-marie for about 30 minutes in the oven at 180°C, 350°F, Gas Mark 4.

SAUCE HOLLANDAISE

Serves 4-6
2-3 tablespoons lemon juice
2 egg yolks
100 g (4 oz) unsalted butter, melted and cooled
salt
white pepper
pinch of sugar (optional)

**Preparation time: 5 minutes
Cooking time: 15 minutes**

Sauce hollandaise can be served with vegetables, poached fish and poached eggs.

1. Place 1 tablespoon of the lemon juice in a bowl with the egg yolks. Put over a pan of hot water, taking care that the water does not touch the base of the bowl. Beat well until the mixture thickens.
2. Add the butter, a little at a time, beating constantly. If necessary remove the bowl from the pan now and again so that the mixture does not become too hot.
3. When all the butter has been added, add salt, pepper and the remaining lemon juice. If the lemons are very sharp, a pinch of sugar may be required.
4. Keep warm over a pan of hot, but not boiling, water.

Variation:
Salted butter can be used for this sauce, but a creamier, less salty sauce can be achieved with unsalted butter.

> When made to accompany the Terrine de champignons the sauce should be very lemony – adjust the amount of lemon juice accordingly. If the lemons are very sharp, add a pinch of sugar.

TERRINE DE RIS DE VEAU
Pork and Veal Terrine with Sweetbreads

Serves 8-12
100 g (4 oz) sweetbreads
4 tablespoons white wine
2 tablespoons brandy
75 g (3 oz) butter
1 onion, peeled and finely chopped
1 garlic clove, peeled and crushed
350 g (12 oz) lean minced pork
350 g (12 oz) minced veal
1 egg, beaten
salt
freshly ground black pepper
pinch of nutmeg
225 g (8 oz) thinly sliced streaky bacon rashers, rinded

Preparation time: 20-30 minutes, plus soaking, marinating and cooling
Cooking time: 1 hour 40 minutes
Oven: 190°C, 375°F, Gas Mark 5

1. Soak the sweetbreads in cold water for 1-2 hours.
2. Drain the sweetbreads, place in a pan of boiling salted water and blanch for 2-3 minutes. Drain again and place in a bowl of cold water, then remove the membranes.
3. Slice the sweetbreads, put into a bowl with the wine and brandy, and leave to marinate for 1-2 hours.
4. Melt 25 g (1 oz) of the butter in a small pan, add the onion and cook until soft but not coloured.
5. Mix the garlic with the onion, and place in a bowl with the minced pork, veal and egg. Add salt, pepper, nutmeg and the sweetbread marinating liquor. Mix well.
6. Line a 1 kg (2 lb) terrine with the streaky bacon rashers. Place a layer of the pork mixture in the bottom of the terrine. Put the sliced sweetbreads on top and cover with the remainder of the pork mixture. Cover the top with streaky bacon rashers.
7. Put the terrine in a bain-marie or roasting tin of hot water. Place in a preheated oven and cook for about 1½ hours. The terrine is cooked when it has shrunk slightly from the sides of the dish and the surrounding fat and juices are clear, not pink.
8. When cooked, cool for 30 minutes, then cover with a piece of greaseproof paper or foil and place a weight on top. (A 1 kg (2 lb) bag of sugar is ideal.) Leave until completely cold and set.
9. Melt the remaining butter in a pan and pour over the top of the terrine. F To serve, cut into 1 cm (½ inch) slices and serve with French bread and salad.
F It will keep unopened for 5-7 days in a refrigerator, or 1 month in the freezer. Thaw overnight in the refrigerator.

FLAKY PASTRY

100 g (4 oz) plain flour
pinch of salt
40 g (1½ oz) butter or hard margarine
40 g (1½ oz) lard or white fat
4-5 tablespoons water

Preparation time: 20 minutes, plus resting
Oven: as given in recipes

As the pastry needs to be cool all the time it is being made, it should be chilled for approximately 30 minutes between rollings in warm weather.

1. Sift the flour and salt into a bowl. Add half the butter or margarine and, using a round-ended knife or palette knife, chop finely. Rub the fat into the flour with the fingertips. Add sufficient water to bind the dough together to a soft but not sticky consistency.
2. Flour a pastry board lightly and shape the dough into a rectangle about 41 cm (16 inches) long. Ease any rounded corners into shape. Mark lightly into thirds.
3. Using a round-bladed knife, dab half the lard or white fat on the top two-thirds of the pastry, leaving a border around the edge.
4. Fold the lower third up over the centre section, then fold the top third down over this, keeping the corners square. Seal the edges with the rolling pin and give the pastry a half turn so that the fold is at the right hand side.
5. Roll out the pastry as before and repeat the process, first using the remaining butter or margarine and then the remaining lard or white fat.
6. Roll and fold once more without the addition of any fat.
7. Wrap in cling film or put in a polythene container with a lid. Chill for 20 minutes or longer before use. [F]
[F] Flaky pastry can be frozen, wrapped in polythene. Defrost for 2-3 hours in a refrigerator or cool room.

Quantity guide			
plain flour	100 g (4 oz)	175 g (6 oz)	225 g (8 oz)
salt	pinch	pinch	¼ teaspoon
butter or margarine	40 g (1½ oz)	50 g (2 oz)	75 g (3 oz)
lard or white fat	40 g (1½ oz)	50 g (2 oz)	75 g (3 oz)
water	4-5 tablespoons	6-7 tablespoons	150 ml (¼ pint)

RISSOLES AU CRABE
Crab Turnovers

Makes 10-12
15 g (½ oz) butter
15 g (½ oz) plain flour
65 ml (2½ fl oz) milk
50 g (2 oz) crab meat, flaked
50 g (2 oz) Gruyère cheese, grated
salt
freshly ground black pepper
100 g (4 oz) Flaky pastry
1 egg, beaten

Preparation time: 10 minutes
Cooking time: 20-25 minutes
Oven: 230°C, 450°F, Gas Mark 8

These tasty turnovers are delicious for light meals, or you can serve them with drinks. They can also be eaten cold on picnics.

1. Melt the butter in a small pan, add the flour and cook for 2-3 minutes, stirring. Add the milk, stirring all the time. Bring to the boil and cook for a further 2-3 minutes.
2. Remove from the heat, stir in the crab meat, cheese, salt and pepper. Allow to cool.
3. Roll out the pastry thinly on a lightly floured board. Cut out 7.5 cm (3 inch) rounds. Brush the edges with beaten egg.
4. Place a small spoonful of the crab mixture in the centre of each round of pastry. Fold over and seal well. Knock up the edges and place on a wetted baking sheet. Brush with beaten egg. [A]
5. Place in a preheated oven and cook for 10-15 minutes until crisp and golden brown. Best served hot.
[A] Can be made earlier in the day and stored in the refrigerator until required. Reheating is not advised.

TOP TO BOTTOM: Rissoles au crabe;
Rissoles au jambon et deux salades

RISSOLES AU JAMBON ET DEUX SALADES
Crisply Fried Bacon with Two Salads

2 heads chicory, cut into rings
½ curly endive, shredded
50 g (2 oz) butter or good pork dripping
225-350 g (8-12 oz) gammon steak, rinded and cut into short strips
Dressing:
6 tablespoons olive oil
3 tablespoons lemon juice
salt
freshly ground black pepper

Preparation time: 15 minutes
Cooking time: 5-8 minutes

1. To make the dressing, mix or shake the oil, lemon juice, salt and pepper together.
2. Toss the chicory and endive separately in the vinaigrette dressing. Place the chicory and endive on opposite sides of individual plates.
3. Melt the butter or dripping in a frying pan, add the gammon and fry quickly over a high heat until golden brown and crisp.
4. Quickly place some of the bacon in the centre of each plate and pour over any fat in the pan. Serve immediately while the bacon is still sizzling.

CRÊPES AUX FRUITS DE MER
Seafood Pancakes

Serves 4-8
300 ml (½ pint) Crêpe batter
225 g (8 oz) haddock or cod, skinned and boned
150 ml (¼ pint) white wine
4 scallops
50 g (2 oz) butter, plus extra for greasing
1 medium onion, peeled and finely chopped
100 g (4 oz) button mushrooms, thinly sliced
1 teaspoon lemon juice
salt
white pepper
25 g (1 oz) plain flour
about 150 ml (¼ pint) milk
4 tablespoons double or whipping cream
100 g (4 oz) peeled prawns
4 tablespoons grated Gruyère cheese
To garnish:
8 whole prawns
finely chopped fresh parsley (optional)

Preparation time: 20 minutes
Cooking time: 40-45 minutes, including making pancakes
Oven: 200°C, 400°F, Gas Mark 6

1. Make 4 large pancakes or 8 smaller ones and keep hot (see Crêpes recipe).
2. Place the haddock in a pan with the white wine and poach over a gentle heat for 10-12 minutes.
3. Cut the scallops into 4 and add to the pan. Cook for a further 2-3 minutes. Drain, reserving the liquor. Flake the haddock and reserve.
4. Meanwhile, melt 25 g (1 oz) of the butter in a pan, add the onion and cook gently until soft but not coloured.
5. Melt the remaining butter in another pan and add the mushrooms, lemon juice, salt and pepper. Cover and cook for a few minutes until soft.
6. When the onions are soft, add the flour. Cook for 1-2 minutes, stirring, then add the fish cooking liquor and milk. Bring to the boil and cook for 2-3 minutes, stirring.
7. Add the cream, haddock, scallops, mushrooms and prawns. Reheat, and thin the sauce if necessary with a little more milk. Taste and adjust the seasoning.
8. Place some of the mixture on each pancake. Roll up and place in a buttered ovenproof dish. Sprinkle the cheese over the top.
9. Place in a preheated oven and cook for 7-10 minutes or under a preheated hot grill to allow the cheese to melt.
10. Serve hot, garnished with the whole prawns and chopped parsley, if liked.

CRÊPES
Pancakes

Serves 4-8
150 g (5 oz) plain flour
¼ teaspoon salt
2 eggs
300 ml (½ pint) milk
1 tablespoon oil
oil, for cooking

Preparation time: 10 minutes
Cooking time: 15-20 minutes

1. Sift the flour and salt into a bowl and make a well in the centre. Break in the eggs and add 150 ml (¼ pint) of the milk. Beat in the flour from the sides of the bowl until a smooth thick batter is obtained. Gradually add the remaining milk. [A]
2. Heat a little oil in a frying pan, then pour it off, leaving a very thin coating on the base of the pan. Pour in sufficient batter to cover the base of the pan thinly, tipping the pan from side to side to spread the batter all over the bottom of the pan.
3. When bubbles appear on the surface, and the underside has browned nicely, turn the pancake over with a spatula and cook on the other side for 1-2 minutes. [A] [F]
4. Make the rest in the same way, re-oiling the pan and reheating it again for each one.
5. To keep hot, place a saucer, rounded side up, on a large plate over a pan of simmering water. As the pancakes are cooked, drape them over the saucer. If they are to be kept for some time or are to be reheated, cover the plate with a bowl.
[A] Either the batter or the pancakes can be made earlier in the day.
[F] Pancakes can be frozen, sandwiched between sheets of greaseproof paper. If many are needed, defrost at room temperature. A few can be defrosted and reheated over hot water as above. Once they have been taken out of the freezer and separated, they defrost very quickly.

Variation:
In France, Brittany especially, pancakes are often made with buckwheat flour which has a lovely nutty flavour. Make in the same way, substituting buckwheat flour for plain flour. Allow the batter to stand for at least 30 minutes.

LEFT TO RIGHT: Crêpes aux fruits de mer; Potage de légumes froids

POTAGE DE LÉGUMES FROIDS
Chilled Vegetable Soup

225 g (8 oz) tomatoes, skinned and chopped
150 g (5 oz) cucumber, peeled and chopped
40 g (1½ oz) spring onions, trimmed and finely chopped
50 g (2 oz) green or red peppers, cored, seeded and chopped
1-2 garlic cloves, peeled and crushed
2 tablespoons fresh white breadcrumbs
1½ tablespoons red wine vinegar
3 tablespoons olive oil
300 ml (½ pint) chicken stock
1 tablespoon chopped fresh basil or good pinch of dried basil
pinch of dried oregano
salt
freshly ground black pepper
5 tablespoons single cream

Preparation time: 30 minutes, plus marinating overnight

1. Place the tomatoes, cucumber, spring onions and peppers in a bowl with the garlic, breadcrumbs, vinegar, oil and stock. Add half the fresh basil or a good pinch of dried basil, the oregano, salt and pepper.
2. Cover and leave to marinate overnight in the refrigerator.
3. The next day, purée the soup in a liquidizer or pass through a fine vegetable mill. Strain through a sieve and add the cream. Taste and adjust the seasoning.
4. Pour the soup into a tureen. Sprinkle with the rest of the fresh basil, or if none is available, some chopped parsley. Serve well chilled.

SAUTÉS & GRILLS

LOTTE À L'ARMORICAINE
Breton-Style Monkfish

4 tablespoons olive oil or other well-flavoured oil
2 medium onions, peeled and finely chopped
2 garlic cloves, peeled and crushed
450-750 g (1-1½ lb) monkfish, cut into 2.5-4 cm (1-1½ inch) slices
2 teaspoons plain flour
350 g (12 oz) tomatoes, skinned, seeded and chopped
150 ml (¼ pint) water or 1 × 400 g (14 oz) can tomatoes, with juice
150 ml (¼ pint) white wine
1 tablespoon brandy
bouquet garni
good pinch of cayenne pepper
good pinch of curry powder
pinch of sugar
salt
freshly ground black pepper
To garnish:
finely chopped parsley

Preparation time: 20 minutes
Cooking time: 30 minutes

1. Heat the oil in a pan, add the onions and garlic and cook until soft but not coloured. Remove from the pan.
2. Add the fish to the pan. Cook for 2-3 minutes until both sides are lightly browned, then remove.
3. Return the onions and garlic to the pan and add the flour. Mix in well and add the tomatoes, water if used, wine, brandy, bouquet garni, cayenne pepper, curry powder, sugar, salt and pepper. The sauce should have a slightly hot, spicy flavour but remember that it will reduce during the cooking, accentuating the flavour.
4. Return the fish to the pan, cover and cook gently for about 20 minutes until the fish is tender. Place the fish on a serving dish.
5. Reduce the sauce, if necessary, until thick enough to coat the back of a spoon. Taste and adjust the seasoning and pour over the fish. Sprinkle with chopped parsley.
6. Serve with rice or new potatoes for a main course.

Variation:
Other fish such as cod, haddock or halibut can be cooked in the same way.

COQUILLES ST JACQUES EN BROCHETTE
Scallop Kebabs

8 large or 16 small scallops
8 streaky unsmoked bacon rashers, rinded
1 egg, beaten
2 tablespoons fine white breadcrumbs
25 g (1 oz) butter, melted
lemon wedges, to serve

Preparation time: 25 minutes
Cooking time: 10-15 minutes

1. Wash the scallops and cut out any black threads. Take off the coral and cut the white meat of large scallops in half.
2. Stretch the bacon rashers with the back of a knife and cut each in half. Wrap a piece of bacon around each piece of white scallop meat.
3. Dip the coral pieces into the egg and coat with breadcrumbs. Brush with melted butter.
4. Arrange the pieces of scallop on skewers, alternating the white meat and the coral.
5. Place under a preheated moderately hot grill or over a barbecue and cook for 10-15 minutes, turning occasionally, until the fish is cooked and golden brown.
6. Serve with lemon wedges and plain boiled rice, a rice pilaff or sauté potatoes. If liked, serve also with melted butter.

Scallops are usually bought still attached to the flat scallop shell. The white scallop is surrounded by a beard-like fringe which must be scraped off. Then remove the black intestinal thread. Slide the blade of a sharp knife under the scallop and carefully ease off the white flesh and the coral.

TOP TO BOTTOM: Lotte à l'Armoricaine;
Coquilles St Jacques en brochette

RAIE AU BEURRE NOIR
Poached Skate with Black Butter

4 wings of skate, about 225 g (8 oz) each
1 small onion, peeled and sliced
1 bay leaf
1 sprig thyme
1 sprig parsley
3 tablespoons white wine vinegar
salt
freshly ground black pepper
50 g (2 oz) butter
2 tablespoons capers
1 tablespoon finely chopped fresh parsley

Preparation time: 5 minutes
Cooking time: 25 minutes

1. Place the fish in a large pan. Add the onion, bay leaf, thyme, parsley and 1 tablespoon of the wine vinegar. Cover with water and add salt and pepper. Cover and poach for about 20 minutes until the fish is tender.
2. Remove carefully from the pan and drain well. Take off the skin and, if possible, the large bones at the top of each piece of skate. Keep hot.
3. Slowly melt the butter in a pan and cook until dark nutty brown. Pour on the remaining wine vinegar.
4. Sprinkle the capers and chopped parsley over the fish. Strain the sauce over the fish and serve immediately with plain boiled potatoes.

> In spite of its name, black butter should be a dark nutty brown, not black. It is best made with clarified butter, which will ensure that there are no dark, gritty specks in the sauce from the milk solids in the butter.
>
> To make 50 g (2 oz) clarified butter, melt 100 g (4 oz) butter in a small pan over low heat. Cook without stirring until the butter begins to foam. Skim off the foam, remove from the heat and let it stand until the milky deposits have sunk to the bottom, leaving a clear yellow liquid.

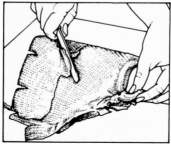
Removing the skin

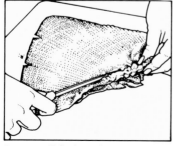
Cutting off the large bone

FILETS DES PLIES AU PAMPLEMOUSSE
Fillets of Plaice with Grapefruit

225 g (8 oz) small new or old potatoes, scraped or peeled
salt
white pepper
8 fillets plaice, skinned, about 750 g (1½ lb)
2 tablespoons seasoned flour
50 g (2 oz) butter
150 ml (¼ pint) grapefruit juice
1 egg yolk
½ teaspoon sugar
1 tablespoon water

Preparation time: 10 minutes
Cooking time: 30-35 minutes

1. Place the potatoes in a steamer over a pan of boiling water. Add salt and a little white pepper, cover and cook for 30-35 minutes until tender. Slice and keep hot.
2. Meanwhile, fold each plaice fillet into 2 or 3 depending on the size. Coat with seasoned flour.
3. Melt the butter in a frying pan or flameproof dish, add the fillets and cook for 1-2 minutes on each side to colour slightly.
4. Pour over the grapefruit juice, bring to the boil, cover and cook for 5-6 minutes. Arrange on a serving dish and keep hot.
5. Beat the egg yolk in a small bowl with the sugar and water. Place over a pan of hot water and cook gently, beating all the time, until the sauce is thick enough to coat the back of a spoon. Taste and adjust the seasoning.
6. Pour the sauce over the fish. Arrange the sliced potatoes down each side of the fish. Serve hot.

Variation:
This delicately flavoured dish could equally well be made with other white fish fillets, such as sole or whiting. If liked, garnish with a little grapefruit or lemon zest, sprinkled on top of the sliced potatoes.

LEFT TO RIGHT: Raie au beurre noir; Cabillaud à la Niçoise

CABILLAUD À LA NIÇOISE
Mediterranean-Style Cod

---

4 cod cutlets, about 225 g (8 oz) each
2 tablespoons seasoned flour
4 tablespoons oil
2 medium onions, peeled and finely chopped
2 garlic cloves, peeled and crushed
450 g (1 lb) tomatoes, skinned, seeded and chopped
150 ml (¼ pint) dry white wine
2 sprigs fresh fennel
2 small sprigs fresh thyme
1 bay leaf
salt
freshly ground black pepper
pinch of sugar
about 50 g (2 oz) green olives

Preparation time: 15 minutes
Cooking time: 20-25 minutes

1. Coat the cod in the seasoned flour. Heat the oil in a pan, add the fish and cook on both sides until browned. Remove from the pan.
2. Add the onions and garlic to the pan and cook until soft but not coloured. Add the tomatoes, white wine, fennel, thyme, bay leaf, salt, pepper and sugar.
3. Return the fish to the pan, cover and cook gently for about 15 minutes until the fish is just tender.
4. Take the fish from the pan and carefully remove the skin and bones. Place on a hot serving dish.
5. Add the olives to the sauce. (The number of olives depends on personal taste.) Cook the sauce for a further 5 minutes, or until it is thick enough to coat the back of a spoon.
6. Pour the sauce over the fish and serve hot with rice or new potatoes.

ENTRECÔTE AUX ESCHALLOTES
Sirloin Steaks with Shallots

50 g (2 oz) butter
6 shallots, peeled and finely chopped or 2 small onions,
   peeled and finely chopped
4 sirloin steaks, 175-225 g (6-8 oz) each
salt
freshly ground black pepper
1 tablespoon oil
2 tablespoons brandy
150 ml (¼ pint) red wine
To garnish:
finely chopped fresh parsley

Preparation time: 10 minutes
Cooking time: 10-15 minutes

1. Melt the butter in a pan, add the shallots or onions and cook until soft.
2. Sprinkle the steaks on both sides with salt and pepper.
3. Heat the oil in a frying pan. For a rare steak, quickly sear the meat on both sides over a high heat. For medium rare or well done steaks, reduce the heat once the steaks are browned and cook according to preference.
4. Remove the steaks from the pan and place on a hot serving dish. Keep hot.
5. Add the shallots or onions and butter to the frying pan, add the brandy and wine and cook over a high heat until the sauce reduces slightly. Taste and adjust the seasoning.
6. Pour the sauce over the steaks, sprinkle with chopped parsley and serve at once.

STEAK AU POIVRE
Peppered Steak

25 g (1 oz) black or white peppercorns, coarsely crushed
4 rump or entrecôte (sirloin) steaks, 175-225 g (6-8 oz)
   each
50 g (2 oz) butter
1-2 tablespoons brandy
150 ml (¼ pint) dry white wine
4 tablespoons double or whipping cream
salt
chopped fresh parsley, for sprinkling

Preparation time: 5 minutes
Cooking time: 10-15 minutes

1. Press the crushed peppercorns well into each side of the steaks. A potato masher is ideal for this.
2. Melt the butter in a pan, add the steaks and cook for 1-2 minutes on each side or according to preference.
3. Pour off any surplus butter, retaining all the peppercorns in the pan. Warm the brandy by pouring it into a jug and placing this in hot water for 1 minute. Pour over the steaks and carefully ignite.
4. Remove the steaks from the pan and place on a hot serving dish. Keep hot.
5. Add the wine to the pan, bring to the boil and cook until it has reduced by half. Pour in the cream, mix well and reheat without boiling. Add salt to taste.
6. Pour the sauce over the steaks and serve at once with sauté potatoes.

> **Green peppercorns** can also be used for this dish. These are the unripe fresh corns, available bottled or canned in brine or vinegar, or even freeze-dried.
> **White peppercorns** come from corns picked when ripe, when they turn red. The outer skin is removed, and they are then dried.
> **Black peppercorns** are the unripe corns, picked when still green. They are dried in the sun and their outer covering is left on. Black peppercorns are milder than the white ones and are considered to have a more aromatic flavour.

BOEUF STROGANOFF
Steak with Soured Cream

75 g (3 oz) butter
2 medium onions, peeled and thinly sliced
175 g (6 oz) button mushrooms, thinly sliced
450-750 g (1-1½ lb) fillet of beef or rump steak, trimmed,
   cut into 5 mm × 5 cm (¼ inch × 2 inch) strips
2 tablespoons brandy
1 tablespoon plain flour
salt
freshly ground black pepper
150 ml (¼ pint) red wine
150 ml (¼ pint) soured cream
To garnish:
chopped fresh parsley

Preparation time: 20 minutes
Cooking time: 10-15 minutes

If soured cream is not available, stir 1 tablespoon of lemon juice into 150 ml (¼ pint) double cream and leave for about 30 minutes.

1. Melt 40 g (½ oz) of the butter in a pan, add the onions and cook gently until soft and golden brown. Add the mushrooms to the pan and cook for 3-4 minutes. Remove from the pan.
2. Heat the remaining butter in the pan, add the meat and fry briskly for 3-4 minutes.
3. Warm the brandy by pouring it into a jug and placing this in hot water for 1 minute. Pour over the meat and carefully ignite.
4. Return the mushrooms and onions to the pan with the flour and cook, stirring, for 1 minute. Add salt, pepper and wine. Bring to the boil and simmer for 1-2 minutes until the sauce reduces slightly.
5. Add the soured cream and heat through without boiling.
6. Pour into a hot serving dish and sprinkle with chopped parsley. Serve with rice.

> Be careful not to let the sauce come to the boil once you have added the sour cream, or the sauce will curdle.

LEFT TO RIGHT: Steak au poivre;
Entrecôte aux eschallotes

CÔTES DE PORC À L'ORANGE
Pork Chops in Orange Sauce

25 g (1 oz) butter
4 pork chops, about 175 g (6 oz) each, rinds removed
150 ml (¼ pint) orange juice
salt
freshly ground black pepper
pinch of fresh chopped or powdered thyme
To garnish:
1 orange, thinly sliced
chopped fresh parsley (optional)

Preparation time: 10 minutes
Cooking time: 25-30 minutes

To make this dish more decorative, cut the skin of the orange with a canelle knife before slicing it.

1. Melt the butter in a pan, add the chops and fry for 7-10 minutes on each side until completely cooked. Remove from the pan with a slotted spoon and place on a heated serving dish. Keep warm.
2. Add the orange juice to the pan and stir to mix in the meat juices adhering to the sides and bottom of the pan. Bring to the boil and simmer until reduced by half. Taste and add salt, pepper and a pinch of thyme.
3. Pour the sauce over the chops. Halve the orange slices and use to garnish the edge of the dish. Sprinkle the chops with parsley, if using.

CÔTES DE PORC NORMANDE
Normandy Pork

50 g (2 oz) butter
4 pork steaks, about 100-175 g (4-6 oz) each
1 medium onion, peeled and finely chopped
1 large cooking apple, peeled, cored and chopped
1 tablespoon plain flour
300 ml (½ pint) dry cider
salt
freshly ground black pepper
4 tablespoons double or whipping cream
To garnish (optional):
1-2 eating apples, peeled, cored and cut into 1 cm
   (½ inch) slices
25 g (1 oz) butter

Preparation time: 15 minutes
Cooking time: 30 minutes

ESCALOPES DE VEAU À LA CRÈME
Escalopes of Veal in Cream Sauce

50-75 g (2-3 oz) butter
1 medium onion, peeled and finely chopped
100 g (4 oz) button mushrooms, sliced
salt
white pepper
4 escalopes veal, about 75-100 g (3-4 oz) each, trimmed
1-2 tablespoons seasoned flour
150 ml (¼ pint) dry white wine
150 ml (¼ pint) double or whipping cream
freshly chopped parsley, to garnish

Preparation time: 15 minutes
Cooking time: 20-25 minutes

1. Melt half the butter in a pan, add the onion and cook until soft but not coloured. Add the mushrooms and cook until tender. Remove from the pan.
2. Coat the escalopes in seasoned flour. Melt the remaining butter in the pan, add the escalopes and cook for 4-5 minutes on both sides until tender. Remove from the pan and keep hot.
3. Return the onion and mushrooms to the pan. Stir in 2 teaspoons of seasoned flour. Mix well, add the wine and bring to the boil.
4. Remove the pan from the heat and stir in the cream. Taste and adjust the seasoning. Warm through, being careful not to let the sauce boil, and pour over. Sprinkle with chopped parsley and serve.

1. Melt the butter in a pan, add the pork steaks and cook for 7-10 minutes on both sides until cooked and golden brown. Remove from the pan with a slotted spoon and place on a heated serving dish. Keep warm.
2. Add the onion to the pan and cook gently until soft, then add the apple and cook for 1-2 minutes. Stir in the flour and cook for a further 1-2 minutes, then add the cider and bring to the boil, stirring all the time. Add salt and pepper and simmer for about 15 minutes or until the apple is soft.
3. Beat the sauce well to blend in the apple. Add the cream and heat through without boiling. Pour over the meat.
4. To make the garnish, if using, melt the butter in a pan, add the apple slices and cook gently on both sides until soft and golden brown. Arrange down the centre of the dish on top of the sauce.

TOP TO BOTTOM: Côtes de porc à l'orange;
Escalopes de veau à la crème

ROGNONS D'AGNEAU
À LA LIÈGEOISE
Liège-Style Kidneys

8-12 lamb's kidneys, skinned, halved and cored
350 g (12 oz) new potatoes
salt
50 g (2 oz) butter
freshly ground black pepper
1 teaspoon juniper berries, coarsely crushed
2 tablespoons brandy
65 ml (2½ fl oz) white stock
2 tablespoons double or whipping cream
To garnish:
finely chopped fresh parsley

Preparation time: 20 minutes, plus soaking
Cooking time: 30 minutes

1. Soak the kidneys in cold water for 30 minutes.
2. Place the potatoes in a pan of boiling salted water and cook for 7-10 minutes. Drain well.
3. Melt 25 g (1 oz) of the butter in a pan, add the potatoes and cook until golden brown. Remove from the pan. Keep hot.
4. Drain the kidneys and dry on paper towels. Season with pepper only.
5. Melt the remaining butter in the pan, add the kidneys and cook quickly for 5-7 minutes until just tender. Take care not to overcook or cook them slowly, as they will become tough. Sprinkle with salt and place on a hot serving dish. Keep hot.
6. Add the juniper berries to the pan with the brandy and stir well to incorporate the meat juices. Add the stock, bring to the boil and simmer for a few minutes to reduce slightly. Add the cream and reheat, being careful not to let it come to the boil. Taste and adjust the seasoning.
7. Strain the sauce over the kidneys. Arrange the potatoes on the dish and sprinkle the kidneys with chopped parsley. Serve hot.

TRANCHES DE GIGOT
AUX HERBES DE PROVENÇE
Lamb with Provençal Herbs

1-1½ tablespoons chopped fresh thyme, rosemary and powdered savory
3 tablespoons olive oil
salt
freshly ground black pepper
4 slices leg of lamb, about 225-275 g (8-10 oz) each or 4 double lamb chops, trimmed
40 g (1½ oz) butter
2 tablespoons brandy (optional)
150 ml (¼ pint) red or rosé wine or stock
sprigs of fresh herbs, to garnish (optional)

Preparation time: 10 minutes, plus marinating
Cooking time: 20-25 minutes

Ask your butcher to cut the leg of lamb slices for you, leaving the centre bone in.

1. Mix the herbs with 2 tablespoons of the oil. Sprinkle the meat with salt and pepper and spread the herb mixture over the surface. (The amount of herbs used depends on personal preference.) Leave for 4-5 hours.
2. Heat the butter and remaining oil in a pan, add the meat and cook for 7-10 minutes on both sides until tender.
3. Pour off all but 1 tablespoon of fat from the pan. Warm the brandy, if using, by pouring it into a jug and placing this in hot water for 1 minute. Pour over the meat and carefully ignite.
4. Remove the meat from the pan with a slotted spoon and arrange on a hot serving dish. Keep hot.
5. Reheat the fat and juices in the pan, pour in the wine or stock and boil for a few minutes to reduce by half. Taste and adjust the seasoning.
6. Pour the sauce over the meat. Garnish with sprigs of fresh herbs, if liked.

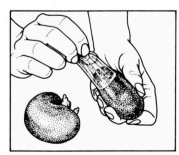
Skinning the kidney

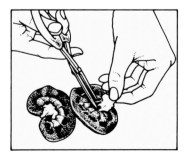
Snipping out the core with scissors

LEFT TO RIGHT: Rognons d'agneau à la Liègeoise;
Tranches de gigot aux herbes de Provence; Poulet au citron

POULET AU CITRON
Lemony Chicken

---

4 small poussins
150 ml (¼ pint) fresh lemon juice
salt
freshly ground black pepper
100 g (4 oz) butter, melted
1 teaspoon sugar, if liked
To garnish:
1 lemon, cut into wedges
1 bunch watercress

Preparation time: 15 minutes, plus marinating
Cooking time: 40 minutes

If small poussins are not available, buy 2 small chickens, 750 g-1 kg (1½-2 lb) each. Cook in the same way but allow extra time for grilling. Serve half a bird to each person.

1. Using a pair of scissors, cut the chickens down the backbone. Place on a board, flatten well and skewer through the legs to keep them flat. Sprinkle with a little lemon juice, salt and pepper. Leave for 1-2 hours.
2. Brush the chickens well with melted butter and place under a preheated moderately hot grill. Take care not to have the pan too close to the grill or the skin on the chicken will burn. Cook the birds for 7-10 minutes on one side, then brush again with butter and cook the other side for the same time. Turn over once again, brush with butter and cook until the skin is crisp and the chicken tender. Arrange on a hot serving dish.
3. Mix the remaining butter and lemon juice with the juices in the grill pan. Add salt and pepper. Add a little sugar, to taste, if the lemon juice makes the sauce seem too sharp.
4. Pour the sauce over the chicken. Garnish with lemon wedges and watercress.

MAIN MEALS

PAUPIETTES DE BOEUF À LA PAYSANNE
Country-Style Beef Rolls

175 g (6 oz) pork sausage meat
1 small onion, peeled and finely chopped
2 garlic cloves, peeled and crushed
1 tablespoon finely chopped fresh parsley
salt
freshly ground black pepper
4 thin slices topside or buttock steak, about 75-100 g
    (3-4 oz) each, trimmed
50 g (2 oz) dripping or vegetable fat
225 g (8 oz) carrots, peeled and sliced
150 g (5 oz) turnips, thickly peeled and diced
1 large onion, peeled and thinly sliced
2 sticks celery, diced
1 teaspoon plain flour
4 tomatoes, skinned, seeded and chopped
225 ml (7½ fl oz) red wine
225 ml (7½ fl oz) beef stock
225 g (8 oz) French beans, trimmed and halved
350-450 g (12 oz-1 lb) small new or firm old potatoes
chopped fresh parsley

Preparation time: 30-40 minutes
Cooking time: 1¾-2¼ hours
Oven: 180°C, 350°F, Gas Mark 4

1. Mix the sausage meat with the onion, 1 of the crushed garlic cloves, the parsley, salt and pepper.
2. Divide the mixture into 4 and spread a portion on each slice of beef. Roll up neatly and tie with string.
3. Melt dripping in a flameproof casserole and brown the paupiettes. Remove from the pan.
4. Add the carrots, turnips, sliced onion, celery and garlic to the pan and cook gently until soft.
5. Stir in the flour and tomatoes and mix well. Return paupiettes to the pan. Add the wine, stock, salt and pepper. Cover, place in a preheated oven and cook for 1½-2 hours until tender.
6. Cook the French beans and potatoes in boiling salted water. Drain well.
7. Remove the strings from the paupiettes and arrange on a heated serving dish. Remove vegetables from the sauce and arrange these around the dish, with the beans and potatoes. Keep hot.
8. Bring the sauce to the boil and reduce until thick enough to coat the back of a spoon. Pour over the paupiettes and sprinkle with chopped parsley.

BOEUF EN DAUBE PROVENÇAL
Provençal Beef Stew

1 kg (2 lb) lean chuck or blade-bone, trimmed and cut into
    4 cm (1½ inch) cubes
2-3 onions, peeled and sliced
3 carrots, peeled and sliced
1 strip orange peel, without pith
1 bay leaf
4-5 peppercorns
300 ml (½ pint) red wine
50 g (2 oz) dripping or vegetable fat
2-3 garlic cloves, peeled and crushed with a little salt
300 ml (½ pint) beef stock
salt
freshly ground black pepper
To garnish:
finely chopped fresh parsley

Preparation time: 20 minutes, plus marinating overnight
Cooking time: 2-2½ hours
Oven: 160°C, 325°F, Gas Mark 3

1. Place the meat in a deep dish with 1 sliced onion, the carrots, orange peel, bay leaf and peppercorns. Pour on the red wine, cover and leave to marinate in the refrigerator overnight.
2. Remove the meat and vegetables from the wine and drain well, reserving the marinade.
3. Heat the dripping in a flameproof casserole, add the meat and brown on all sides. Remove from the pan with a slotted spoon.
4. Add the remaining onions and the crushed garlic to the pan and cook gently until golden brown.
5. Return the meat to the pan, together with the wine, vegetables, orange peel and bay leaf used in the marinade. Discard the peppercorns. Add the stock, salt and pepper. Bring to the boil.
6. Cover tightly, place in a preheated oven and cook for 2-2½ hours until tender.
7. Discard the bay leaf and skim any fat from the surface of the sauce. Remove the meat from the pan and boil the sauce until reduced by half.
8. Return the meat to the casserole or place in another dish and pour the sauce over. Sprinkle with finely chopped parsley.
9. Serve with rice or creamed potatoes.

LEFT TO RIGHT: Boeuf en daube Provençal;
Paupiettes de boeuf à la paysanne

BOEUF À LA BOURGUIGNONNE
Burgundy Beef Stew

40-50 g (1½-2 oz) dripping or vegetable fat
100 g (4 oz) piece rindless streaky bacon, diced
225 g (8 oz) small onions, peeled
750 g (1½ lb) chuck or buttock steak, trimmed and cut
    into 2.5 cm (1 inch) cubes
2 garlic cloves, peeled and crushed
25 g (1 oz) plain flour
300 ml (½ pint) red wine
150 ml (¼ pint) beef stock
2 teaspoons tomato purée
salt
freshly ground black pepper
1 bouquet garni
175 g (6 oz) button mushrooms, quartered
finely chopped fresh parsley, to garnish

Preparation time: 15 minutes
Cooking time: 2½-3 hours
Oven: 160°C, 325°F, Gas Mark 3

1. Melt the dripping in a flameproof casserole, add the bacon and fry until golden brown. Remove from the pan with a slotted spoon.
2. Add the onions to the pan and cook until golden brown. Remove from the pan with a slotted spoon.
3. Add a little more dripping if necessary and heat. Add the meat in batches and brown well on all sides. Return all the meat to the pan and add the garlic and flour. Cook for 4-5 minutes over a gentle heat until the flour is lightly browned.
4. Return the bacon and onions to the pan and add the red wine, stock and tomato purée. Bring to the boil, stirring all the time. Add salt, pepper and the bouquet garni.
5. Cover, place in a preheated oven and cook for 2-2½ hours until tender.
6. Thirty minutes before the end of the cooking time, add the mushrooms to the pan. Taste and adjust the seasoning. [A] [F]
7. To serve, remove the bouquet garni and skim any fat from the surface. Sprinkle with chopped parsley and serve with rice.
[A] Can be prepared in advance and reheated for about 30 minutes at 200°C, 400°F, Gas Mark 6.
[F] Thaw in a refrigerator or cool room overnight.

Small pickling onions are best for this dish and can be cooked whole. Peel them carefully, leaving as much stalk and root on as possible so that they stay whole during cooking. If small ones are not available, use larger ones cut in quarters.

TOURNEDOS EN CROÛTE
Fillet Steak in Pastry

40 g (1½ oz) butter
1 tablespoon oil
2 small onions, peeled and finely chopped
1 garlic clove, peeled and crushed (optional)
100 g (4 oz) mushrooms, finely chopped
salt
freshly ground black pepper
pinch of nutmeg
4 fillet steaks, about 175 g (6 oz) each, trimmed
225 g (8 oz) Flaky pastry (page 20) or 450 g (1 lb) frozen
    puff pastry
4 slices ham
1 egg, beaten
fresh chervil or parsley sprigs, to garnish

Preparation time: 30 minutes, plus cooling, and resting pastry
Cooking time: 30-35 minutes
Oven: 220°C, 425°F, Gas Mark 7

1. Heat 25 g (1 oz) of the butter and the oil in a pan, add the onions and garlic and cook until soft but not coloured. Add the mushrooms, salt, pepper and nutmeg and stir over a gentle heat until the mushrooms are cooked and all the moisture has evaporated.
2. Turn out on to a plate and divide into 8 portions. Leave to cool.
3. Heat the remaining butter in a frying pan, add the steaks and sear on both sides. Cool quickly and keep chilled until required.
4. Roll out the pastry and cut into 8 rounds large enough to half cover the steaks. Brush a 2.5 cm (1 inch) border around the edge of each pastry round with beaten egg.
5. Cut the ham into 8 rounds the same size as the steaks.
6. Take 4 of the pastry rounds and place one piece of ham on each round. Cover the ham with a portion of the mushroom mixture, a fillet steak, another portion of mushrooms and another ham round.
7. Finally, cover with another circle of pastry. Seal well and knock up the edges. Cut leaves from the pastry trimmings and arrange 3 in the centre of each croûte.
8. Leave to rest in the refrigerator for about 30 minutes.
9. Brush the pastry with beaten egg to glaze. Place in a preheated oven and cook for about 20 minutes until golden brown. Serve garnished with a sprig of chervil or parsley.

TOP TO BOTTOM: Boeuf braisé à la ménagère;
Boeuf à la Bourguignonne; Tournedos en croute

BOEUF BRAISÉ À LA MÉNAGÈRE
Braised Beef

Serves 4-6

40 g (1½ oz) dripping or vegetable fat
1.5 kg (3 lb) topside, silverside, top rump or top rib beef,
   trimmed and tied
12 small onions, peeled, or 3 medium onions, peeled and
   cut into quarters
2 large carrots, peeled and cut into fingers
2 teaspoons plain flour
225 ml (7½ fl oz) red wine
225 ml (7½ fl oz) beef stock or water
1 tablespoon tomato purée
salt
freshly ground black pepper
1 bay leaf
To garnish:
finely chopped fresh parsley (optional)

Preparation time: 20 minutes
Cooking time: 1½-1¾ hours
Oven: 190°C, 375°F, Gas Mark 5

1. Melt the dripping in a flameproof casserole, add the meat and brown on all sides. Remove from the pan with a slotted spoon.
2. Add the onions and carrots to the pan and cook until lightly browned. Stir in the flour, mix well and cook for a further 3-4 minutes, until the flour also is lightly coloured. Add the red wine, stock or water and tomato purée. Bring to the boil gently, stirring all the time. Add salt and pepper and bay leaf.
3. Replace the meat on top of the vegetables. Cover, place in a preheated oven and cook for 1¼-1½ hours or until the meat is tender. Discard bay leaf.
4. Remove the meat, slice it and arrange on a heated serving dish. Adjust the seasoning of the sauce. Arrange the vegetables around the meat and pour a little of the sauce over. ⅌
5. Sprinkle with chopped parsley, if liked, and serve the rest of the sauce in a gravy boat.
⅌ Any leftover meat slices could be packed in foil or boiling bags with some of the sauce, preferably in individual portions, and frozen. Reheat from frozen.

TRUITES À L'ESTRAGON
Trout with Tarragon

4 trout, 175-225 g (6-8 oz) each, cleaned
3 tablespoons fresh white breadcrumbs
2 tablespoons chopped fresh tarragon
salt
freshly ground black pepper
1 egg, beaten
1 small onion, peeled and sliced
150 ml (¼ pint) dry white wine
8 sprigs fresh tarragon
25 g (1 oz) butter
1 tablespoon plain flour
150 ml (¼ pint) single cream
fleurons of puff or flaky pastry (optional)

Preparation time: 20-30 minutes
Cooking time: 25-30 minutes
Oven: 190°C, 375°F, Gas Mark 5

1. Remove the backbones from the trout.
2. Mix the breadcrumbs with half the chopped tarragon. Add salt and pepper and bind the mixture together with beaten egg. Spread a layer of the mixture inside each trout and re-form, pressing firmly to mould the shape.
3. Season the outside of the fish and place in an oven-proof dish with the onion and wine. Place a sprig of tarragon on each trout. Cover with foil.
4. Place in a preheated oven and cook for about 20 minutes until tender.
5. Remove the trout from the dish, reserving the cooking liquor. Carefully remove the heads, tails and skin, and place the fish on a hot serving dish.
6. Strain the cooking liquor and, if necessary, make up to 150 ml (¼ pint) with water.
7. Melt the butter in a pan, add the flour and cook for 1-2 minutes. Add the cooking liquor and bring to the boil, stirring all the time. Add the cream, stirring, and bring to the boil again. Add salt, pepper and the remaining chopped tarragon.
8. Blanch the remaining sprigs of tarragon by plunging them briefly into a pan of boiling water.
9. Pour the sauce over the fish and garnish with tarragon and the fleurons of pastry, if used.

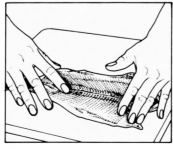

Slitting down the belly　　　Cleaning and opening out

SAUMON EN PAPILLOTE
Salmon in Foil

4 salmon steaks, about 175 g (6 oz) each
oil, for brushing
1-2 tablespoons lemon juice
1-2 teaspoons chopped fresh herbs
salt
freshly ground black pepper
50 g (2 oz) butter

Preparation time: 10 minutes
Cooking time: 20-25 minutes
Oven: 200°C, 400°F, Gas Mark 6

1. Scrape the scales from the skin of the salmon, wash well and dry with paper towels.
2. Brush 4 squares of foil lightly with oil. Place a piece of salmon on each. Sprinkle with lemon juice, herbs, salt and pepper. Add a knob of butter.
3. Draw up the foil and pinch the edges together to seal well. Transfer to a baking sheet. Place in a preheated oven and cook for 20-25 minutes.

AÏOLI
Garlic Mayonnaise

3-4 cloves garlic, peeled
¼ teaspoon salt
2 egg yolks
300 ml (½ pint) oil, preferably olive oil
2-3 tablespoons lemon juice
white pepper

Preparation time: 15 minutes

1. Crush the garlic to a smooth paste with the salt.
2. Beat in the egg yolks.
3. Gradually add the oil a few drops at a time, in the same way as making Mayonnaise (page 16). When the sauce thickens, add 1 tablespoon lemon juice.
4. Continue adding the oil and finally add the remaining lemon juice and pepper to taste.

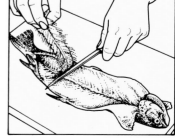

Pressing down backbone　　　Removing backbone

TOP TO BOTTOM: Saumon en papillote; Truites à l'estragon

BOURRIDE
Fish Stew

Serves 4-6

1 kg (2 lb) firm white fish, trimmed and cut into large
 pieces
350-450 g (12 oz-1 lb) firm potatoes, peeled and thickly
 sliced
2 egg yolks
300 ml (½ pint) Aïoli (page 38)
6-8 slices French bread, toasted or fried
fresh parsley sprigs, to garnish

Court bouillon:

600 ml (1 pint) water
150 ml (¼ pint) dry white wine
1 medium onion, peeled and sliced
1 small leek, trimmed and sliced
1 slice lemon
1 sprig parsley
1 sprig fennel
1 sprig thyme
350 g (12 oz) fish trimmings
1 teaspoon salt
6 black peppercorns

Preparation time: 30 minutes
Cooking time: 1¼-1½ hours

This dish is really considered to be a soup, but is so
substantial, it can be served as a main dish. Any firm
white fish can be used. Use the trimmings and heads
of the fish for the Court bouillon.

1. To make the Court bouillon, put the water, wine,
onion, leek, lemon, parsley, fennel, thyme, fish
trimmings, salt and peppercorns into a pan, bring to
the boil and simmer for 45 minutes. Strain.
2. Place the pieces of fish and potatoes in the Court
bouillon. Cover, bring gently to the boil and simmer
for 15 minutes until the fish and potatoes are
cooked. Carefully lift into a deep serving dish or
soup tureen. Keep hot.
3. Measure the Court bouillon and if necessary make
up to 600 ml (1 pint) with water. Beat the egg yolks
into 150 ml (¼ pint) of the Aïoli. Pour on a little of
the Court bouillon and blend well together. Return to
the pan and cook gently, stirring all the time, until
the sauce is thick enough to coat the back of a spoon.
4. Take care not to boil or the sauce will separate. If
this happens, liquidize the sauce at high speed,
strain into a clean pan and heat through.
5. Pour the sauce over the fish and potatoes.
6. To serve, place 1-2 slices French bread in the
bottom of each hot soup plate. Place a portion of fish
on each piece and some potatoes in the plate. Pour
over some of the sauce and garnish with fresh
parsley. Serve the rest of the Aïoli separately.

SAUTÉ DE PORC CATALANE
Catalan Pork Stew

Serves 4-6
150 ml (¼ pint) oil
750 g (1½ lb) lean pork, cut into 2.5 cm (1 inch) cubes
1 large onion, peeled and sliced
2 garlic cloves, peeled and crushed
450 g (1 lb) tomatoes, skinned and chopped
1 green or red pepper, about 225 g (8 oz), cored, seeded and sliced
1½ teaspoons paprika
150 ml (¼ pint) chicken stock
salt
freshly ground black pepper
1 aubergine, about 350 g (12 oz), sliced
2-3 tablespoons seasoned flour
175-225 g (6-8 oz) long-grain rice, washed and drained

Preparation time: 20 minutes, plus draining
Cooking time: 1¼-1½ hours

1. Heat 2 tablespoons of the oil in a flameproof casserole, add the meat and brown on all sides. Remove from the pan with a slotted spoon.
2. Add the onion and garlic to the pan and cook until soft and golden brown. Return the meat to the pan and add the tomatoes, pepper, paprika, stock, salt and pepper.
3. Bring to the boil, cover with greaseproof paper and a lid, and simmer for approximately 1 hour or until the meat is tender. [A] [F]
4. Meanwhile, sprinkle the aubergine slices with a little salt and leave on a wire tray to drain for at least 30 minutes. Turn occasionally.
5. Wash the aubergine slices and wipe dry with paper towels. Dip in the seasoned flour.
6. Heat some of the remaining oil in a frying pan, add the aubergines and cook until golden brown and tender. Add more oil as required. Keep hot.
7. Place the rice in a large pan of boiling salted water to which 1 tablespoon oil has been added and cook, uncovered, for 10-12 minutes.
8. Drain, refresh and drain well again. Place in a buttered dish. Cover and place in the oven to keep hot.
9. When the pork is cooked, check and adjust the consistency of the sauce and seasoning.
10. Arrange a border of rice on a hot serving dish. Fill the centre with the meat and place the aubergine slices around.
[A] The casserole can be made the day before and kept refrigerated until required. Reheat for about 30 minutes in a preheated oven at 180°C, 350°F, Gas Mark 4.
[F] Thaw overnight in the refrigerator or in a cool room. Reheat as above.

SAUTÉ DE PORC CORIANDRE
Pork with Coriander

2-3 tablespoons oil
750 g (1½ lb) lean pork, cut into 2.5 cm (1 inch) cubes
2-3 tablespoons seasoned flour
1 medium onion, peeled and chopped
2 garlic cloves, peeled and crushed
2 sticks celery, chopped
2 large tomatoes, skinned and chopped
300 ml (½ pint) chicken stock
1 teaspoon coriander seeds, lightly crushed
salt
freshly ground black pepper
1 tablespoon wine vinegar
1 tablespoon soy sauce
1 teaspoon sugar
chopped fresh coriander leaves, to garnish (optional)

Preparation time: 20 minutes
Cooking time: 1½ hours
Oven: 180°C, 350°F, Gas Mark 4

1. Heat the oil in a flameproof casserole. Toss the meat in the seasoned flour, add to the casserole and brown on all sides. Remove from the pan with a slotted spoon.
2. Add the onion, garlic and celery to the pan and cook until soft and golden brown. Add 2 teaspoons of the seasoned flour and cook for 1-2 minutes.
3. Return the pork to the pan together with the tomatoes, stock, coriander seeds, salt and pepper. Cover, place in a preheated oven and cook for about 1 hour until the meat is tender. [A]
4. Remove the meat from the pan and pile on to a hot serving dish.
5. Add the wine vinegar, soy sauce and sugar to the pan and cook for 5-6 minutes until the sauce is of a coating consistency. Taste and adjust the seasoning. Pour over the meat. [F] Garnish with fresh coriander leaves.
[A] Make a few hours in advance and keep refrigerated until required. Reheat for 20-30 minutes at the cooking temperature and finish the dish as recipe.
[F] Thaw in a refrigerator or cool room overnight.

CLOCKWISE FROM THE FRONT: Sauté de porc Catalane;
Jambon au Meursault; Sauté de porc coriandre

JAMBON AU MEURSAULT
Ham in a Wine and Cream Sauce

450 g (1 lb) cooked ham or gammon, sliced
25 g (1 oz) butter
25 g (1 oz) plain flour
150 ml (¼ pint) milk
150 ml (¼ pint) dry white wine
1 tablespoon tomato purée
salt
white pepper
2-3 tablespoons grated Parmesan cheese

Preparation time: 15 minutes
Cooking time: 30 minutes
Oven: 200°C, 400°F, Gas Mark 6

1. Arrange the ham or gammon slices in an oven-proof dish.
2. Melt the butter in a pan, add the flour and cook for 1-2 minutes, stirring. Add the milk and bring to the boil, stirring all the time.
3. Add the wine and bring to the boil again, still stirring. Cook for 1-2 minutes, then stir in the tomato purée, salt and pepper.
4. Pour the sauce over the ham and sprinkle the cheese over the top. [A] [F]
5. Place in a preheated oven and cook for about 20 minutes until hot and browned on the top.
6. Serve with jacket potatoes, if liked.
[A] Can be made earlier in the day and chilled until required.
[F] To freeze, make in a foil container. Cover, label and freeze for up to 1 month.

POTÉE AU CHOU À L'AUVERGNATE
Boiled Meats and Vegetables Auvergne Style

Serves 6-8

1 kg (2 lb) piece lean blade-bone, shoulder or hand of pork
450 g (1 lb) carrots, peeled and cut into fingers
450 g (1 lb) turnips, thickly peeled and cut into large dice
4 medium onions
4 cloves
4-5 sticks celery, cut into short lengths
4-6 small leeks, trimmed
1 large bouquet garni
2 garlic cloves, peeled and crushed with a little salt
salt
freshly ground black pepper
1 small green cabbage, cut into 6 pieces
225 g (8 oz) piece smoked streaky bacon, soaked in cold
   water overnight and drained
450 g (1 lb) continental cooking sausage, cut into 4 cm
   (1½ inch) pieces
750 g (1½ lb) potatoes, peeled and cut into large pieces

Preparation time: 30-40 minutes, plus soaking overnight
Cooking time: 1½-2 hours

1. Place the pork, carrots, turnips and 3 of the onions in a large pan. Stick the cloves in the other onion and add this to the pan with the celery, leeks, bouquet garni and garlic.
2. Cover with water and add salt and pepper. Cover, bring to the boil and simmer gently for 30-40 minutes.
3. Meanwhile, place the pieces of cabbage in boiling salted water and blanch for 3-4 minutes. Drain and refresh under cold running water. Drain well again.
4. Add the cabbage and bacon to the pan. Continue cooking for a further 30 minutes.
5. Add the sausage and potatoes to the pan and cook for another 25-30 minutes, until the meats and vegetables are tender.
6. Remove the bouquet garni and cloves. Taste and adjust the seasoning.
7. Slice the meats and arrange in a hot deep serving dish. Arrange the vegetables around the meat. Pour over a little of the cooking liquor and serve the rest separately, as a sauce.
F Any leftover meat slices (but not the vegetables) could be frozen in a plastic container with a little of the stock. Freeze the remaining stock separately, to be served as a soup. Reheat meat slices and stock from frozen.

LEFT TO RIGHT: Potée au chou à l'Auvergnate; Filet de porc farci

FILET DE PORC FARCI
Stuffed Fillet of Pork

1 pork fillet, about 275-350 g (10-12 oz), trimmed
25 g (1 oz) butter
1 medium onion, peeled and finely chopped
2-3 garlic cloves, peeled and crushed
75 g (3 oz) pork sausage meat
75 g (3 oz) minced lean pork
40 g (1½ oz) fresh white breadcrumbs
2 tablespoons finely chopped fresh parsley
1 teaspoon dried sage
¼ teaspoon salt
freshly ground black pepper
1 egg, beaten
1 gammon rasher
50 g (2 oz) lard or vegetable fat
24 small onions, peeled
225 g (8 oz) carrots, peeled and sliced
25 g (1 oz) butter
salt
300 ml (½ pint) chicken stock

Preparation time: 30-40 minutes
Cooking time: 1½ hours
Oven: 180°C, 350°F, Gas Mark 4

1. Place the fillet on a board and, with the point of a sharp knife, cut down the centre, taking care not to cut right through the meat. Ease the fillet open with the knife held parallel to the board.
2. Make another cut along the mount of meat on one side. Repeat on the other side and open the fillet out, so that you now have a wide piece of meat.
3. Melt the butter in a small pan, add the onion and garlic and cook until soft but not coloured.
4. Mix the sausage meat, minced pork, breadcrumbs, half the parsley, sage, onion, garlic, salt and pepper together in a bowl. Bind with the beaten egg.
5. Place the stuffing down the centre of the gammon rasher and roll up crossways to form a long cigar shape.
6. Place this package down the length of the prepared fillet. Wrap the fillet round the bacon and with a needle and coarse thread, sew up the edges and ends of the fillet. [A]
7. Melt the lard in a flameproof dish or small roasting tin, add the meat and brown on all sides. Cover tightly, place in a preheated oven and cook for about 1½ hours.
8. Meanwhile, place the onions in a pan of boiling salted water and blanch for 7-10 minutes. Drain well.
9. Thirty minutes before the end of the cooking time, add the onions to the meat, turn in the fat and continue cooking.
10. Place the carrots in a pan with the butter, a little salt and just enough water to cover. Cook gently until the carrots are tender and the liquid has evaporated.
11. Remove the meat from the pan, take out the trussing thread and cut into 1 cm (½ inch) slices. Arrange on a heated serving dish, with the onions and carrots.
12. Pour off any surplus fat in the pan and pour in the stock. Stir round well to mix in any of the residue of meat juices adhering to the pan. Bring to the boil and allow to reduce slightly. Taste and adjust the seasoning.
13. Pour some stock over the meat and serve the rest separately. Garnish with remaining chopped parsley.
[A] The meat can be prepared earlier in the day and kept in the refrigerator until required.

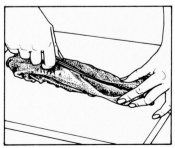
Cutting down the fillet

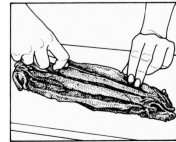
Opening out fillet

CAILLES À L'ORANGE
Quails in Orange Sauce

---

3 small oranges
1 clove
4 peppercorns
50 g (2 oz) butter
65 ml (2½ fl oz) French vermouth
4 quail, cleaned, with legs trussed or skewered with cocktail sticks
salt
pinch of cayenne pepper
4 streaky bacon rashers, rinded
1-2 tablespoons brandy (optional)

Preparation time: 30 minutes
Cooking time: 30 minutes
Oven: 200°C, 400°F, Gas Mark 6

1. Cut 8 thin slices from 1½ oranges, leave 4 slices whole and cut the rest in half. Scoop out any flesh remaining.
2. Grate the rind and squeeze the juice from the remaining 1½ oranges.
3. Pound the scooped-out flesh with a third of the grated rind, the clove, peppercorns, 15 g (½ oz) of the butter, and mix with 1-2 teaspoons of the vermouth. Place a little of this mixture inside each bird.
4. Stretch the rashers of streaky bacon with the back of a knife and wrap one around each bird. Tie or skewer in place. Sprinkle with salt and with cayenne pepper.
5. Melt the remaining butter in a flameproof pan and brown the birds on all sides. Cover, place in a preheated oven and cook for about 20 minutes until tender.
6. When the quail are cooked, warm the brandy by pouring it into a jug and placing this in hot water for 1 minute. Pour over the birds and carefully ignite. Remove the birds from the pan. Keep hot.
7. Pour the remaining vermouth, the orange juice and the rest of the grated rind into the pan. Bring to the boil and cook until the sauce reduces slightly. Taste and adjust the seasoning.
8. Remove the string or skewers from the birds. Place each bird on a whole slice of orange on a hot serving dish. Pour the sauce over and garnish the dish with the half slices of orange down each side.

COQ AU RIESLING
Chicken in Riesling

---

75 g (3 oz) butter
1 oven-ready chicken, about 1.5 kg (3½ lb), jointed into 8 pieces
3 small onions, peeled and finely chopped
300 ml (½ pint) Riesling or other fruity dry white wine
salt
white pepper
175 g (6 oz) button mushrooms
1 teaspoon lemon juice
2-3 tablespoons water
25 g (1 oz) plain flour
2 tablespoons brandy
4 tablespoons double or whipping cream
lemon zest, to garnish (optional)

Preparation time: 20 minutes
Cooking time: 1 hour
Oven: 200°C, 400°F, Gas Mark 6

1. Melt 40 g (1½ oz) butter in a flameproof casserole, add the chicken pieces and brown on all sides. Remove from the pan with a slotted spoon.
2. Add the onions to the pan and cook gently until soft but not coloured. Add the wine and return the chicken to the pan. Bring to the boil, add salt and pepper.
3. Cover, place in a preheated oven and cook for 40-45 minutes until tender. A F
4. Meanwhile, place the mushrooms in a small casserole with 15 g (½ oz) of the butter, the lemon juice, water, salt and pepper. Place in a preheated oven and cook for about 15 minutes.
5. Blend the remaining butter with the flour to make a beurre manié (page 53).
6. When the chicken pieces are cooked, lift them out with a slotted spoon and arrange on a heated serving dish, cover and keep warm.
7. Bring the sauce in the casserole to the boil and whisk in the beurre manié, piece by piece, until the sauce has thickened. Simmer for 3-4 minutes, then add the brandy and cream and reheat without allowing the sauce to boil. Taste and adjust the seasoning.
8. Drain the mushrooms and scatter over the chicken. Pour the sauce over and serve garnished with lemon zest, if liked.
9. Serve with pilaff or plain boiled rice.
A Prepare in advance and keep refrigerated until required. Reheat for 20-30 minutes at 180°C, 350°F, Gas Mark 4 and continue with recipe.
F Thaw in a refrigerator or in a cool room overnight. Reheat and finish recipe as above.

TOP TO BOTTOM: Coq au Riesling; Cailles à l'orange

LAPIN AU CARAMEL
Caramelized Rabbit

1.25-1.5 kg (2½-3 lb) rabbit, jointed
75 g (3 oz) caster sugar
50 g (2 oz) butter
4 tablespoons orange juice
300 ml (½ pint) stock
2 tablespoons oil
100 g (4 oz) piece rindless streaky bacon, diced
1 large onion, peeled and finely chopped
1 garlic clove, peeled and crushed
1 tablespoon plain flour
2 teaspoons tomato purée
grated rind of 1 orange
salt
freshly ground black pepper
1 bouquet garni
3 tablespoons medium dry sherry
3 tablespoons double or whipping cream
To finish:
15 g (½ oz) butter
50-75 g (2-3 oz) green olives (depending on personal
    preference)
finely chopped fresh parsley

Preparation time: 20 minutes
Cooking time: 1¼ hours
Oven: 190°C, 375°F, Gas Mark 5

1. Coat each piece of rabbit with caster sugar. Melt the butter in a pan, add the rabbit and cook until the sugar has caramelized. Remove from the pan.
2. Add the orange juice and a little stock to the pan and stir round well to incorporate any juices or caramel adhering to the pan.
3. In a casserole, heat the oil, add the bacon and cook until golden brown. Remove from the pan.
4. Add the onion and garlic to the pan and cook until soft. Add the flour and cook for 2-3 minutes, then add the remaining stock, orange juice mixture, tomato purée and grated orange rind. Bring to the boil, stirring, and add salt and pepper.
5. Put in the rabbit and bacon and add the bouquet garni. Cover tightly, place in a preheated oven and cook for 45-50 minutes until tender. A F
6. Arrange the rabbit on a heated serving dish.
7. Remove the bouquet garni. Simmer the sauce slightly to reduce if necessary. Add the sherry and cream, and reheat without boiling. Taste and adjust the seasoning, and pour over the rabbit.
8. Melt the remaining butter in a small pan, add the olives and heat through. Scatter the olives and parsley over the top of the rabbit and serve hot.
A Cook a few hours in advance and keep refrigerated until required. Reheat for 20-30 minutes.
F Thaw in a refrigerator or in a cool room overnight.

NAVARIN D'AGNEAU
Lamb Stew

750 g (1½ lb) lean, boneless lamb, cut into cubes
2 teaspoons caster sugar
50 g (2 oz) dripping or vegetable fat
2-3 onions, peeled and thinly sliced
3-4 carrots, peeled and sliced
2 garlic cloves, peeled and crushed
25 g (1 oz) plain flour
300 ml (½ pint) white wine
150 ml (¼ pint) stock
1 tablespoon tomato purée
salt
freshly ground black pepper
350-450 g (12 oz-1 lb) small new potatoes, scraped, or old
    potatoes, peeled and cut into large dice

Preparation time: 20 minutes
Cooking time: 2-2½ hours
Oven: 160°C, 325°F, Gas Mark 3

For a more economical dish, middle neck of lamb can be used – allow another 100 g (4 oz) meat per person. All stock can be used instead of wine and stock.

1. Toss the meat in the sugar.
2. Melt the dripping in a flameproof casserole, add the meat in batches and brown on all sides. Remove from the pan.
3. Add the onions and carrots to the pan and cook gently until golden brown. Add the garlic and cook for a few seconds.
4. Return the meat to the pan, stir in the flour and cook for 2-3 minutes until lightly browned. Add the wine, stock, tomato purée, salt and pepper. Bring to the boil, stirring all the time. Place in a preheated oven, cover and cook for 45 minutes. F
5. Meanwhile, place the potatoes in a pan of boiling salted water and cook for 5-7 minutes. Drain, add to the meat and continue cooking for a further hour or until the meat and potatoes are cooked and tender. A
A Can be cooked in advance and refrigerated overnight, then reheated for 30 minutes at 200°C, 400°F, Gas Mark 6. Do not leave in an unlined cast iron pan.
F This dish will freeze better without the potatoes. Thaw in a refrigerator or cool room overnight and continue with step 5 as above.

LEFT TO RIGHT: Lapin au caramel; Faisan au whisky

FAISAN AU WHISKY
Pheasant with Whisky

Serves 3-4

40 g (1½ oz) butter
1-2 pheasant, depending on size, cleaned and trussed
1 onion, peeled and finely chopped
85-120 ml (3-4 fl oz) whisky
150 ml (¼ pint) beef stock
salt
freshly ground black pepper
pinch of cayenne pepper
4-6 juniper berries
120 ml (4 fl oz) double or whipping cream
½ teaspoon lemon juice
To garnish:
watercress

Preparation time: 15 minutes
Cooking time: 1-1¼ hours
Oven: 190°C, 375°F, Gas Mark 5

A young hen pheasant weighing 1 kg (2 lb) will feed 2-3 people. A large cock bird could weigh up to 1.5-1.7 kg (3½-4 lb) and will feed 4 people.

1. Melt the butter in a flameproof casserole, add the pheasant and brown on all sides. Remove from the pan with a slotted spoon.
2. Add the onion to the pan and cook until soft and golden brown.
3. Warm half the whisky by standing it in a jug of hot water for a few seconds. Return the pheasant to the pan, pour the whisky over and carefully ignite.
4. Pour on the stock and add salt, pepper, cayenne and the juniper berries. Bring to the boil.
5. Place in a preheated oven and cook for 45 minutes–1 hour until tender; an old pheasant will take longer.
6. When the pheasant is tender, remove from the pan and joint it – cut off the legs and divide into 2, remove the breasts and cut in 2. Discard the wings. Arrange the pheasant on a heated serving dish.
7. Boil the sauce until it is syrupy, add the remaining whisky, the cream and lemon juice. Taste and adjust the seasoning, and reheat without allowing the sauce to come to the boil.
8. Strain the sauce over the pheasant, garnish with watercress and serve with green beans.

VENAISON AUX CASSIS
Venison in Blackcurrant Sauce

Serves 4-6
750 g (1½ lb) boneless venison, cut into 2.5 cm (1 inch)
  cubes
1 large onion, peeled and sliced
1 carrot, peeled and sliced
12 peppercorns
2 bay leaves
450 ml (¾ pint) red wine
50 g (2 oz) dripping or vegetable fat
1 tablespoon plain flour
300 ml (½ pint) beef stock
350 g (12 oz) blackcurrants
pinch of sugar
To garnish:
triangular croûtons of fried bread
chopped fresh parsley

**Preparation time: 20 minutes, plus marinating
overnight
Cooking time: 2-3 hours
Oven: 160°C, 325°F, Gas Mark 3**

1. Place the venison in a deep dish with the onion,
carrot, peppercorns, bay leaves and wine. Cover and
leave overnight in the refrigerator to marinate.
2. Remove the meat and vegetables separately from
the marinade and drain. Reserve the red wine and
bay leaves but discard the peppercorns.
3. When the meat is well drained, melt the dripping
in a flameproof casserole, add the meat and brown.
Remove from the pan with a slotted spoon.
4. Add the drained carrot and onion to the pan and
cook for a few minutes. Add the flour and cook for a
further 1-2 minutes, then add the stock, red wine,
bay leaves from the marinade, blackcurrants, salt
and pepper.
5. Cover and cook for 2-3 hours, depending on the
age of the venison, until the meat is tender. [F]
6. Remove the meat carefully from the sauce and
place on a heated serving dish.
7. Purée the sauce in a food processor or liquidizer.
Do not over-purée or the pips in the blackcurrants
become gritty. Strain the sauce into a clean pan. [A]
8. Reheat and, if necessary, boil to reduce until
thick enough to coat the back of a spoon. Taste and
adjust the seasoning, adding the sugar.
9. Pour the sauce over the meat and garnish with the
fried croûtons and chopped parsley.
[A] Make a few hours in advance but reduce sauce
only slightly. Reheat as above.
[F] Thaw in a refrigerator or in a cool room overnight.
Reheat for 20-30 minutes at 180°C, 350°F, Gas Mark
4. Finish the dish as recipe.

TOP TO BOTTOM: Gigot au pistou; Venaison aux cassis

GIGOT AU PISTOU
Leg of Lamb with Garlic Stuffing

1 small leg of lamb, boned
15 g (½ oz) butter
300 ml (½ pint) stock
450 g (1 lb) potatoes, peeled and cut into 5 mm (¼ inch)
  slices
8 small tomatoes
25 g (1 oz) butter
4-5 tablespoons oil
pinch of salt
small sprigs of fresh rosemary
Pistou:
100 g (4 oz) streaky bacon, rinded and finely chopped
3 garlic cloves, peeled and crushed
1½ teaspoons finely chopped fresh basil or ¾ teaspoon
  dried
1 tablespoon finely chopped fresh parsley

**Preparation time: 25 minutes, excluding boning
time
Cooking time: allow 45 minutes per 450 g (1 lb) –
weigh meat after stuffing
Oven: 180°C, 350°F, Gas Mark 4**

1. To make the Pistou, mix the bacon, garlic, basil
and parsley together.
2. Place inside the leg of lamb. Sew up to a neat
shape with a trussing needle and string. [A]
3. Spread the butter over the surface and put in a
roasting tin. Place in a preheated oven and cook for
the calculated time.
4. Meanwhile, place the potatoes in a pan of boiling
salted water and cook for 4-5 minutes. Drain well. [A]
5. With the point of a sharp knife, make a crosswise
cut on top of the tomatoes, cutting just through the
skin. This prevents them splitting badly, when
grilled. Brush with oil. [A]
6. Just before the meat is cooked, heat the butter and
oil in a frying pan, add the potatoes and cook,
turning frequently, until crisp and golden brown.
7. Place the tomatoes under a preheated hot grill
and cook for 4-5 minutes until just cooked – take
care not to overcook. Sprinkle with salt.
8. Remove the strings from the meat and place on a
hot serving dish. If liked, garnish the lamb with
small sprigs of rosemary. Arrange the potatoes down
each side, with the tomatoes at each end.
9. Pour off any excess fat from the pan and pour in
the stock. Bring to the boil, taste and adjust the
seasoning. Serve separately.
[A] The meat and tomatoes can be prepared in
advance and kept refrigerated for a few hours until
required. The potatoes can also be blanched in
advance, but take care to refresh them under cold
running water until they are completely cold.

POULET BASQUAISE
Basque Chicken

4 tablespoons oil
175 g (6 oz) piece rindless smoked streaky bacon, diced
1 oven-ready chicken, about 1.5 kg (3½ lb), jointed into 8 pieces
4 onions, peeled and sliced
2-3 garlic cloves, peeled and crushed
2 medium green peppers, cored, seeded and thickly sliced
¼ teaspoon dried marjoram
350 g (12 oz) juicy tomatoes, skinned, seeded and chopped or 1 × 400 g (14 oz) can tomatoes
150-300 ml (¼-½ pint) chicken stock
salt
freshly ground black pepper

Preparation time: 20 minutes
Cooking time: 1 hour
Oven: 200°C, 400°F, Gas Mark 6

1. Heat the oil in a flameproof casserole, add the bacon and cook until golden brown. Remove from the pan with a slotted spoon.
2. Add the chicken pieces to the pan and brown on all sides. Remove from the pan with a slotted spoon.
3. Add the onions and garlic to the pan and cook gently until nearly soft, then add the peppers and marjoram. Cover and cook gently for 10 minutes.
4. Add the tomatoes and stock – if fresh tomatoes are used, add 300 ml (½ pint) stock, but if canned tomatoes and their juice are used, add only 150 ml (¼ pint) stock. Add salt and pepper.
5. Return the chicken and bacon to the casserole.
6. Place in a preheated oven and cook for 40-45 minutes until the chicken is tender. [A] [F]
7. To serve, arrange the chicken on a hot serving dish. Simmer the sauce if necessary to reduce until it is thick enough to coat the back of a spoon. Taste and adjust the seasoning and pour over the chicken.
[A] Cook in advance and reheat for about 30 minutes at 180°C, 350°F, Gas Mark 4.
[F] Thaw in a refrigerator or in a cool room overnight. Reheat as above.

POULET À LA COMTOISE
Creamy Chicken from the Franche-Comté

75 g (3 oz) butter
1 oven-ready chicken, about 1.5 kg (3½ lb)
3 carrots, peeled and chopped
2 leeks, white part only, trimmed and sliced
1 large onion, peeled and sliced
2 sticks celery, chopped
1.75 litres (3 pints) water
225 g (8 oz) button mushrooms
40 g (1½ oz) plain flour
150 ml (¼ pint) single cream
1 egg yolk
salt
white pepper
2 tablespoons lemon juice
pinch of nutmeg
100 g (4 oz) Gruyère cheese, grated

Preparation time: 30 minutes
Cooking time: 1 hour 35 minutes
Oven: 200°C, 400°F, Gas Mark 6

Reserve the green part of the leeks for making soup.

1. Melt 40 g (1½ oz) of the butter in a large pan, add the chicken and brown gently on all sides. Remove from the pan.
2. Add the carrots, leeks, onion and celery to the pan and cook until soft but not coloured.
3. Return the chicken to the pan and cover with the water. Add salt and pepper, bring to the boil and simmer gently for about 1 hour until tender.
4. When the chicken is nearly cooked, carefully skim off the fat on the surface and place in a clean pan, together with a little of the stock. Cook the mushrooms in this, adding salt and pepper, for 5-7 minutes until tender, shaking the pan occasionally to prevent the mushrooms from sticking to the base of the pan. Drain and keep warm.
5. When the chicken is cooked, remove from the pan and drain. Skin the chicken, joint or slice, cover and keep hot.
6. Liquidize the vegetables in the stock, return to the pan and boil rapidly for 10-15 minutes to reduce to approximately 600 ml (1 pint).
7. Using a knife, blend the remaining butter with the flour to make a beurre manié.
8. When the stock has reduced, add small pieces of the beurre manié, a little at a time, to the boiling stock, whisking constantly. When all the beurre manié has been incorporated and the sauce is smooth, simmer for 3-4 minutes.
9. Mix the cream and egg yolk well together, pour on some of the hot sauce and beat well. Return the egg and cream mixture to the sauce in the pan and reheat, being careful not to allow it to boil. Taste and adjust the seasoning, adding the lemon juice and a pinch of nutmeg.
10. Place the chicken in a heated deep dish, add the mushrooms to the sauce and pour over.
11. Sprinkle the grated cheese over the chicken. Place in a preheated oven and cook for about 10 minutes until the cheese has melted and browned. Serve with boiled rice.

Beurre manié is the classic French method of thickening sauces, casseroles or stews. Work the butter and flour into a smooth paste with a fork or knife. Divide the mixture into little knobs and add them one at a time to the hot liquid, whisking continuously. In a few minutes, the sauce will thicken and become smooth and shiny. Do not let the sauce boil, or it will separate.

Poulet Basquaise

VEGETABLES & SALADS

AUBERGINES À LA PORTUGAISE
Portuguese-Style Aubergines

2 medium aubergines, about 225 g (8 oz) each, cut in half
  lengthways
salt
4-5 tablespoons oil
1 medium onion, peeled and finely chopped
1-2 garlic cloves, peeled and crushed
225 g (8 oz) tomatoes, skinned, seeded and chopped
2 tablespoons seasoned flour
2-3 tablespoons fresh white breadcrumbs
1 tablespoon finely chopped fresh parsley or basil
freshly ground black pepper
butter, for greasing

Preparation time: 20 minutes, plus draining
Cooking time: 40-45 minutes
Oven: 200°C, 400°F, Gas Mark 6

1. Using a sharp knife, remove the stalks and cut round between the flesh and the skin of each aubergine half, being careful not to cut the skin. Score through the flesh in a diamond pattern, sprinkle lightly with salt and place upside down on a wire tray. Allow to drain for at least 30 minutes.
2. Meanwhile, heat 1 tablespoon of the oil in a small pan, add the onion and garlic and cook until soft but not coloured. Add the tomatoes and cook gently for 10-15 minutes.
3. Wash the aubergines and dry them on paper towels. Heat the remaining oil in a frying pan. Dip the cut sides of the aubergines in seasoned flour, add to the pan and fry gently on both sides until tender right through. Remove from the pan.
4. Carefully scrape out the flesh from each aubergine half with a spoon, being careful not to damage the skin. Place the flesh in a bowl and mix with the tomato mixture and sufficient breadcrumbs to give a firm consistency. Add parsley, salt and pepper.
5. Fill the aubergine skins with the mixture and place in a buttered ovenproof dish. Sprinkle the tops with a few breadcrumbs and a little oil. [A] [F]
6. Place under a preheated hot grill or in a preheated oven and cook for about 20 minutes until heated through and browned.
[A] Can be prepared in advance and reheated.
[F] Place on foil tray, wrap in cling film and pack in a polythene bag. Reheat in the oven from frozen, allowing 40-45 minutes.

FENOUIL À LA NIÇOISE
Mediterranean-Style Fennel

4 medium fennel bulbs, trimmed
2 tablespoons oil
2 medium onions, peeled and finely chopped
2 garlic cloves, peeled and crushed with a little salt
350 g (12 oz) tomatoes, skinned, seeded and chopped
¼ teaspoon chopped fresh thyme
1 bay leaf
150 ml (¼ pint) chicken stock
salt
freshly ground black pepper
50 g (2 oz) black olives, stoned
75 g (3 oz) Gruyère cheese, grated

Preparation time: 25 minutes
Cooking time: about 1¼ hours
Oven: 180°C, 350°F, Gas Mark 4;
then: 200°C, 400°F, Gas Mark 6

1. Place the fennel bulbs in a pan of boiling, salted water and cook for about 20 minutes. Drain, refresh under cold running water and drain well again. Cut each bulb in halves or quarters.
2. Heat the oil in a pan, add the onions and garlic and cook until soft but not coloured. Add the tomatoes, thyme, bay leaf, stock, salt and pepper. Cover and cook over a gentle heat for 10-15 minutes. Remove the bay leaf.
3. Place the fennel and olives in a casserole. Coat with the sauce. Cover, place in a preheated oven and cook for 30-40 minutes or until the fennel is quite tender.
4. Sprinkle the cheese over the top. Increase the oven temperature and cook, uncovered, for a further 10 minutes until the cheese has melted and browned. Alternatively, place under a preheated hot grill and brown.

LEFT TO RIGHT: Fenouil à la Niçoise; Aubergines à la Portugaise

AUBERGINE AU PARMESAN
Aubergine with Parmesan Cheese

Serves 4-5 as a vegetable dish, 2-3 as a lunch dish
1 aubergine, about 350 g (12 oz), sliced
salt
6-8 tablespoons oil
1-2 beaten eggs
3 hard-boiled eggs, sliced
100 g (4 oz) Gruyère cheese, thinly sliced
2 tablespoons grated Parmesan cheese
Sauce:
2 tablespoons oil
1 large onion, peeled and finely chopped
1-2 garlic cloves, peeled and crushed
450 g (1 lb) tomatoes, skinned, seeded and chopped, with
    150 ml (¼ pint) water, or 1 × 400 g (14 oz) can tomatoes
freshly ground black pepper
1 bouquet garni
good pinch of sugar

Preparation time: 45 minutes, plus draining
Cooking time: 40-45 minutes
Oven: 200°C, 400°F, Gas Mark 6

This dish is excellent as a light lunch or supper dish, or as an accompaniment to grilled steaks and chops.

1. Place the sliced aubergine on a wire tray and sprinkle lightly with salt. Allow to drain for at least 30 minutes.
2. To make the sauce, heat the oil in a pan, add the onion and garlic and cook until soft but not coloured. Add the tomatoes and the water or the canned tomatoes and their juice, salt, pepper, bouquet garni and sugar. Bring to the boil and simmer for 20-25 minutes until the sauce thickens. Remove the bouquet garni. Taste and adjust the seasoning.
3. Wash the aubergine slices and dry them on paper towels. Heat the oil in a frying pan. Dip the aubergine slices into the egg, add to the pan and fry until soft and golden brown. Remove from the pan and drain on paper towels.
4. In a deep serving dish, arrange alternate layers of sliced hard-boiled egg, aubergine and sliced cheese. Pour the tomato sauce over and sprinkle the Parmesan cheese over the top. A
5. Place in a preheated oven and cook for 15-20 minutes until heated through and golden brown on top.
A Prepare earlier in the day and reheat as recipe.

CASSEROLE AUX CONCOMBRES
Cucumber Casserole

40 g (1½ oz) butter
2 medium onions, peeled and finely chopped
225 g (8 oz) small new potatoes, scraped
150 ml (¼ pint) chicken stock
salt
freshly ground black pepper
1 cucumber, peeled and cut into thick slices
175 g (6 oz) button mushrooms, halved or quartered if
    large
225 g (8 oz) tomatoes, skinned and quartered
pinch of sugar
chopped fresh parsley or dill, to garnish

Preparation time: 25 minutes
Cooking time: 30 minutes

1. Melt the butter in a heavy-based pan, add the onions and cook gently until soft but not coloured. Cut any large potatoes into cubes, but leave the small ones whole. Add the potatoes, stock, salt and pepper to the pan. Bring to the boil, cover and cook for 10 minutes.
2. Add the cucumber slices and mushrooms. Simmer for another 10 minutes, then add the tomatoes and sugar. Cook for a few more minutes until the vegetables are tender.
3. Pile into a hot deep serving dish, sprinkle with the parsley and/or dill. Serve hot.

HARICOTS VERTS À L'AIL
French Beans in Garlic Sauce

450 g (1 lb) French beans, trimmed and cut in half
salt
225 ml (7½ fl oz) single cream
3 garlic cloves, peeled and crushed
white pepper
chopped fresh chervil or parsley, to garnish

Preparation time: 10 minutes
Cooking time: 20-25 minutes

1. Cook the beans in a pan of boiling, salted water for 10-15 minutes until just tender. Drain well.
2. Meanwhile, place the cream and garlic in a pan and boil for about 7 minutes or until the cream thickens.
3. Add the beans, mix well together and cook for a further 4-5 minutes. Add salt and pepper.
4. Pour into a hot serving dish and sprinkle with chopped chervil or parsley.

PETITS POIS AU LARD
Peas with Bacon

25 g (1 oz) butter
100 g (4 oz) streaky bacon rashers, rinded and cut into
  strips
1 bunch spring onions, trimmed and left whole
450 g (1 lb) shelled or frozen peas
4-5 lettuce leaves, coarsely shredded
salt
freshly ground black pepper
¼ teaspoon sugar

Preparation time: 10 minutes
Cooking time: 30 minutes

1. Melt the butter in a pan, add the bacon and cook until crisp and golden brown. Add the onions and cook for a few seconds, then add the peas and lettuce. Mix well together.
2. Just cover the peas with water and add salt, pepper and sugar. Cover and simmer gently for 20-25 minutes until the vegetables are soft. Taste and adjust the seasoning.
3. Strain into a hot serving dish and pour a little of the cooking liquor over the top.

CLOCKWISE FROM THE FRONT: Aubergine au Parmesan; Haricots verts à l'ail; Casserole aux concombres

CHAMPIGNONS À LA CRÈME ET PAPRIKA
Mushrooms in Cream and Paprika Sauce

50 g (2 oz) butter
350 (12 oz) button mushrooms, halved or quartered if large
25 g (1 oz) plain flour
300 ml (½ pint) milk
65 ml (2½ fl oz) single cream
salt
white pepper
1-2 teaspoons paprika
finely chopped fresh parsley, to garnish

Preparation time: 10 minutes
Cooking time: 20 minutes

1. Melt the butter in a pan, add the mushrooms and cook gently until almost tender.
2. Add the flour to the pan and cook for 1-2 minutes, then add the milk and cream, stirring all the time. Bring to the boil.
3. Add salt, pepper and paprika to taste and cook gently for another 10-15 minutes, stirring occasionally.
4. Pour into a hot serving dish and sprinkle with a little paprika and parsley.

TOMATES ITALIENNES
Italian Tomatoes

4 large tomatoes, halved
2 tablespoons oil
1 medium onion, peeled and finely chopped
2 garlic cloves, peeled and crushed
3-4 tablespoons fresh white breadcrumbs
1-2 tablespoons finely chopped fresh basil or parsley
salt
freshly ground black pepper
50 g (2 oz) Gruyère cheese, grated
fresh basil sprigs, to garnish

Preparation time: 15 minutes
Cooking time: 15 minutes
Oven: 200°C, 400°F, Gas Mark 6

1. Scoop a little flesh from the centre of each tomato half.
2. Heat the oil in a pan, add the onion and garlic and cook until soft but not coloured. Add the breadcrumbs, basil or parsley, salt and pepper.
3. Pile this mixture on top of each tomato and cover with grated cheese. Place in an ovenproof dish. A
4. Place in a preheated oven and cook for 10-15 minutes until the tomatoes are just cooked and the cheese brown. If necessary, finish browning under a preheated grill. Garnish with fresh basil sprigs.
A The tomatoes can be prepared in advance.

SALSIFIS AU BEURRE
Buttered Salsify

---

2 teaspoons plain flour
2 tablespoons lemon juice
1 teaspoon salt
2-3 tablespoons water
450 g (1 lb) salsify, peeled and cut into 5 cm (2 inch)
   lengths
50 g (2 oz) butter
freshly ground black pepper
finely chopped fresh parsley

Preparation time: 15 minutes
Cooking time: 50 minutes-1 hour

1. Blend the flour with the lemon juice, salt and water. Strain into a pan of water and bring to the boil, stirring all the time.
2. Add the salsify, cover and cook for about 30-40 minutes until tender. Drain well.
3. Melt the butter in a pan, add the salsify and brown lightly.
4. Place in a hot serving dish and sprinkle with pepper and chopped parsley.

MANGETOUT À LA PAYSANNE
Mangetout Country-Style

---

450 g (1 lb) mangetout, trimmed, strings removed
salt
100 g (4 oz) piece streaky bacon without rind, cut into dice
40 g (1½ oz) butter
3 tablespoons double or whipping cream
freshly ground black pepper
To garnish:
chopped chives

Preparation time: 15 minutes
Cooking time: 15 minutes

1. Place the mangetout in a pan of boiling salted water and cook for 3-4 minutes or until just tender. Drain well.
2. Meanwhile, cook the bacon in a little of the butter until crisp and golden brown. Remove from the pan with a slotted spoon and drain on paper towels. Keep hot.
3. Melt the remaining butter in the pan in which the bacon was cooked and toss the mangetout in this. Pile into a hot serving dish and keep hot.
4. Just before serving, heat the cream and add the bacon, salt and pepper. Pour over the mangetout and sprinkle with chopped chives.

CHOU FARCI
Stuffed Cabbage

Serves 4-8
8 large cabbage leaves
1 onion, peeled and sliced
1 carrot, peeled and sliced
2 streaky bacon rashers, rinded and diced
1 bay leaf
300 ml (½ pint) stock
1 teaspoon arrowroot
Stuffing:
2 tablespoons oil
1-2 garlic cloves, peeled and crushed (optional)
1 large onion, peeled and finely chopped
350 g (12 oz) lean minced beef
75 g (3 oz) green or red peppers, cored, seeded and diced
1 × 400 g (14 oz) can tomatoes, drained, juice reserved
salt
freshly ground black pepper
pinch of grated nutmeg
2-3 tablespoons fresh white breadcrumbs

Preparation time: 30 minutes
Cooking time: 1½-1¾ hours
Oven: 190°C, 375°F, Gas Mark 5

1. Place the cabbage leaves in a pan of boiling water for 2-3 minutes. Drain well and refresh under cold running water. Dry each leaf carefully and cut out the thick stalk.
2. To make the stuffing, heat the oil in a pan, add the garlic and onion and cook until soft but not coloured. Add the mince and continue cooking over a high heat until the meat has changed colour.
3. Add the peppers, tomatoes, salt, pepper and nutmeg and simmer gently for about 30 minutes until the mince is tender and the mixture is quite dry. Stir in the breadcrumbs. Adjust seasoning.
4. Place a portion of the mixture on each cabbage leaf and fold up to form a parcel. Tie with thin string.
5. Place the sliced onion, carrot and bacon in the bottom of a casserole. Place the cabbage on top.
6. Heat the stock and reserved tomato juice together and pour over the cabbage. Add salt, pepper and bay leaf. Cover with greaseproof paper and a lid. Place in a preheated oven and cook for 45 minutes-1 hour.
7. Remove the cabbage parcels from the pan with a slotted spoon, drain well on paper towels and remove the strings. Arrange in a serving dish.
8. Remove the bay leaf and strain the cooking liquor into a clean pan (if desired purée the vegetables in a liquidizer and add to the cooking liquor). Dissolve the arrowroot with a little water, add to the pan and bring to the boil, stirring. Adjust seasoning.
9. Pour over the cabbage and serve hot.

Chou farci; Carottes forestières (page 62)

CAROTTES FORESTIÈRES
Forester's Carrots

450 g (1 lb) carrots, peeled and thinly sliced
50 g (2 oz) butter
¼ teaspoon sugar
1 garlic clove, peeled and crushed
150 ml (¼ pint) stock
salt
freshly ground black pepper
175 g (6 oz) mushrooms, sliced
chopped fresh parsley, to garnish

Preparation time: 15 minutes
Cooking time: 30 minutes

1. Place the carrots in a pan with 25 g (1 oz) of the butter, the sugar, garlic, stock, salt and pepper. Simmer gently for about 15 minutes until the carrots are almost cooked and most of the liquid has evaporated.
2. Add the mushrooms with the remaining butter. Mix gently together and continue to simmer until the mushrooms are cooked and all the liquid has evaporated. Taste and adjust the seasoning.
3. Turn the mixture over gently, so that the carrots are coated in butter, then pile into a hot serving dish. Sprinkle with chopped parsley.

CÉLERI-RAVE EN PURÉE
Puréed Celeriac

1 large celeriac, about 450 g (1 lb), thickly peeled and cut into large dice
1 tablespoon vinegar or lemon juice
salt
25-50 g (1-2 oz) butter, plus extra for greasing
freshly ground black pepper

Preparation time: 10 minutes
Cooking time: 20-25 minutes

This mixture is much softer than creamed potato and must be well drained before it is puréed. It is an excellent accompaniment to venison.

1. Peel the celeriac and cut into large dice. Plunge at once into a bowl of water with the vinegar or lemon juice, otherwise it will quickly turn brown.
2. Cook the celeriac in a pan of boiling salted water for 20-25 minutes until tender.
3. Drain well and purée. Beat in the butter and add salt and pepper.
4. Place in a hot buttered serving dish.

SALADE PROVENÇALE
Provençal Salad

Serves 4-6
1 medium onion, peeled and thinly sliced
1 teaspoon caster sugar
1 tablespoon wine vinegar
6-8 anchovy fillets, cut into strips
1-2 tablespoons milk (optional)
¼-½ curly endive or crisp lettuce, coarsely shredded
3 tomatoes, skinned and quartered
100 g (4 oz) cooked French beans, trimmed and halved
50 g (2 oz) black olives, stoned
1 small green or red pepper, cored, seeded and diced
¼ cucumber, thinly sliced
2-3 hard-boiled eggs, cut into wedges
Dressing:
1-2 garlic cloves, peeled and crushed with salt
4 tablespoons olive oil
2 tablespoons lemon juice
1 tomato, peeled, seeded and sieved
salt
freshly ground black pepper

Preparation time: 20 minutes, plus marinating

1. Place the onion rings in a bowl. Sprinkle with the caster sugar and vinegar and leave to marinate for about 30 minutes.
2. If the anchovies are very salty, soak them in the milk for 10-15 minutes, then drain on paper towels.
3. Place the endive in a bowl. Place the tomatoes, beans, olives, pepper, cucumber and anchovies on top, tossing them together.
4. Drain the onion rings and reserve the vinegar.
5. To make the dressing, place the garlic in a bowl and gradually beat in the oil. Beat in the lemon juice, vinegar from the onion and puréed tomato. Add salt and pepper to taste.
6. Alternatively, the dressing can be made in a liquidizer. Place the crushed garlic, oil, lemon juice and vinegar and the tomato, cut into quarters, into a liquidizer and switch on to high speed for a few seconds. Strain and add salt and pepper.
7. Pour the dressing over the salad. Arrange the egg wedges on top and the onion rings sprinkled over.

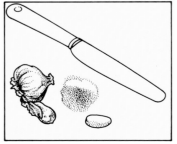
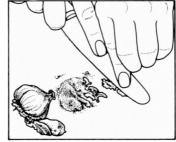

Use a knife and salt   Crushing the garlic

Salade Provençale

CHOU ROUGE AIGRE-DOUX
Sweet and Sour Red Cabbage

25 g (1 oz) butter, plus extra for greasing
1 medium onion, peeled and finely chopped
450 g (1 lb) red cabbage, finely shredded
1 large cooking apple, peeled, cored and chopped
1 tablespoon demerara sugar
2 teaspoons lemon juice
1 tablespoon vinegar
½ teaspoon salt
freshly ground black pepper
1 teaspoon caraway seeds (optional)

Preparation time: 15 minutes
Cooking time: 1¼ hours

1. Melt the butter in a pan, add the onion and cook until soft but not coloured. Add the cabbage, stir round in the butter and cook gently for 2-3 minutes.
2. Add the apple and sugar and stir over a gentle heat for about 10 minutes until the juices run from the cabbage and apple. Add the lemon juice, vinegar, salt, pepper, and caraway seeds, if using.
3. Place a piece of buttered greaseproof paper on top of the cabbage. Cover with a tight fitting lid and cook over a gentle heat for about 1 hour until the cabbage is tender. Shake the pan occasionally to prevent the contents sticking to the bottom of the pan. Taste and adjust the seasoning.
4. Pile into a hot serving dish. Serve hot.

SALADE COMPOSÉE
Mixed Salad

100 g (4 oz) small new potatoes, cooked, refreshed in cold water and sliced
50 g (2 oz) cooked or canned sweetcorn
100 g (4 oz) green or red peppers, cored, seeded and chopped
50 g (2 oz) button mushrooms, thinly sliced
2 sticks celery, sliced
75-100 g (3-4 oz) thick slice of ham, diced
75 g (3 oz) Gruyère or other firm cheese, diced
50 g (2 oz) radishes, sliced
100 g (4 oz) eating apples, peeled, cored and sliced
40 g (1½ oz) shelled hazelnuts
Dressing:
1 teaspoon Dijon mustard
2 tablespoons wine vinegar
4 tablespoons olive or other well flavoured oil
salt
freshly ground black pepper

Preparation time: 20 minutes

1. Place the potatoes, sweetcorn, peppers, mushrooms, celery, ham, cheese, radishes and apples in a large bowl.
2. Mix together the mustard, vinegar, oil, salt and pepper, and pour over the salad. Toss well together.
3. Scatter the hazelnuts over the top.

Variation:
Any cooked or raw vegetables can be used in this salad to give a colourful contrast. Try sliced raw fennel, grated carrot, small florets of raw cauliflower, courgettes, diced and blanched for 2-3 minutes in boiling salted water, or cooked peas, young broad beans, French beans or diced artichoke hearts.

SALADE AU FROMAGE
Cheese Salad

Serves 4-6
100 g (4 oz) white grapes, halved and seeded
100 g (4 oz) Gruyère or other firm cheese, diced
50 g (2 oz) walnuts, roughly chopped
175 g (6 oz) white cabbage, finely shredded
4 small tomatoes, quartered
150 ml (¼ pint) Mayonnaise (page 16)
1 bunch watercress

Preparation time: 20 minutes

SALADE AUX AVOCATS
Avocado Salad

Serves 4-6
1 small lettuce, coarsely shredded
¼ curly endive, coarsely shredded
2-3 tomatoes, skinned and cut into quarters
1 avocado, peeled, stoned and diced
2 tablespoons lemon juice
100 g (4 oz) streaky bacon rashers, rinded and cut into strips
Dressing:
1 teaspoon Dijon mustard
2 tablespoons wine vinegar
4 tablespoons oil
salt
freshly ground black pepper
To garnish:
6-8 tablespoons oil, for frying
2 slices of bread, 1 cm (½ inch) thick, diced

Preparation time: 20 minutes

1. Place the lettuce, endive and tomatoes in a large salad bowl.
2. Toss the diced avocado in the lemon juice, then sprinkle on top of the salad.
3. Fry the bacon in a pan in its own fat until crisp and golden brown. Remove from the pan with a slotted spoon and add to the salad.
4. Mix together the mustard, vinegar, oil, salt and pepper. Pour into the bottom of the salad bowl.
5. Heat the oil in a frying pan, add the diced bread and fry until golden brown. Remove with a slotted spoon and drain on paper towels.
6. Just before serving, toss the salad and sprinkle the croûtons over the top.

1. Mix the grapes, cheese, walnuts, cabbage and tomatoes together with the Mayonnaise.
2. Pile into a serving bowl and garnish with watercress.

Variations:
Use black grapes instead of white for a more colourful salad.
Include a small onion, roughly chopped, in the salad and garnish with finely chopped chives, instead of watercress.

CLOCKWISE FROM THE FRONT: Salade de fromage; Salade composé; Salade aux avocats

SALADE DE CHOU À LA CRÈME
Cabbage Salad with Cream Dressing

1 young green cabbage, finely shredded, or 450 g (1 lb)
   young spring greens, finely shredded
salt
75 g (3 oz) seedless raisins
freshly ground black pepper
150 ml (¼ pint) double or whipping cream
1 tablespoon Dijon mustard
1 tablespoon white wine vinegar
good pinch of cumin seeds

Preparation time: 20 minutes, plus draining

1. Sprinkle the cabbage or greens with a little salt. Allow to drain for 1-2 hours, then dry in a salad spinner or with paper towels.
2. Mix the cabbage or greens, raisins and pepper together in a salad bowl.
3. Place the cream in a bowl with the mustard and stir in the vinegar; do not beat. Leave for a few minutes until the cream begins to thicken.
4. Pour the cream over the cabbage and sprinkle with a few cumin seeds. Toss the salad just before serving.

HOT PUDDINGS & COLD SWEETS

FRAMBOISES AUX FIGUES
Raspberries with Figs

Serves 4-6
8 fresh figs, peeled, or 1 × 425 g (15 oz) can figs, drained
450 g (1 lb) raspberries
50-75 g (2-3 oz) icing sugar, sifted
2-3 tablespoons lemon juice
150 ml (¼ pint) whipping cream, whipped

Preparation time: 20-30 minutes

1. Purée 350 g (12 oz) of the raspberries and then sieve. Add sugar to taste and flavour with the lemon juice. Pour into individual coupe dishes.
2. Quarter the figs and arrange them on top of the raspberry purée.
3. Spoon a large swirl of cream onto each dish. Decorate with the remaining raspberries, if liked.

Variation:
Place a scoop of vanilla ice cream in each dish under the purée.

SABAYON

4 egg yolks
50 g (2 oz) caster sugar
4-5 tablespoons Marsala
sponge finger biscuits, to serve

Preparation time: 5 minutes
Cooking time: 10 minutes

1. Put the egg yolks into a large bowl with the sugar and Marsala. Mix well together and place over a pan of simmering water. Whisk continuously until the mixture becomes thick and fluffy.
2. Pour into warmed glasses and serve at once accompanied with sponge finger biscuits.

Variations:
Use 3-4 tablespoons sherry with 2-3 tablespoons brandy instead of Marsala, or flavour with grated orange rind and orange juice.

OEUFS À LA NEIGE
Floating Islands

4 eggs, separated
250 g (9 oz) caster sugar
600 ml (1 pint) milk
1-2 drops vanilla essence

Preparation time: 15-20 minutes
Cooking time: 20-30 minutes

1. Place the egg whites in a large bowl and whisk until stiff and dry. Measure out 225 g (8 oz) of the sugar. Whisk 1 tablespoon sugar into the whites and continue to whisk until the egg whites are stiff again. Fold in the rest of the sugar in 2-3 batches, taking care not to overfold.
2. Add vanilla to the milk and heat in a shallow pan – a frying pan is ideal. With 2 dessertspoons carefully mould egg shapes from the meringue and drop them into the simmering milk. Alternatively, drop even-sized spoonfuls of the meringue into the milk. Cook gently for 5-7 minutes until set. Carefully remove with a slotted spoon and drain.
3. Mix the egg yolks well with the remaining 25 g (1 oz) sugar. Pour on the hot milk used for poaching the meringues and stir well. Return the mixture to a saucepan and cook over a gentle heat, stirring continuously, until the mixture is thick enough to coat the back of a spoon. Do not allow the custard to boil or it will curdle. If this should happen, liquidize the custard at high speed for a moment or two.
4. Strain the custard into a serving bowl. Carefully float the meringues on the top and chill well before serving.

LEFT TO RIGHT: Framboises aux figues; Sabayon

TARTE AUX CANNEBERGES ET POMMES
Cranberry and Apple Tart

Serves 6-8

100 g (4 oz) cranberries and 50 g (2 oz) granulated sugar or
1 × 185 g (6½ oz) jar cranberry sauce
225 g (8 oz) cooking apples, or Golden Delicious eating
apples, peeled, cored and chopped
grated rind of ½ lemon
2-3 tablespoons lemon juice
25 g (1 oz) hazelnuts, chopped
75 g (3 oz) soft brown sugar
175 g (6 oz) seedless raisins
¼ teaspoon ground cinnamon
¼ teaspoon ground nutmeg
¼ teaspoon ground ginger
pinch of salt
Pastry:
90 g (3½ oz) butter or hard margarine
50 g (2 oz) lard
250 g (9 oz) plain flour, sifted
1 egg yolk
2-3 tablespoons water
1 egg white, lightly whisked
1 tablespoon caster sugar

Preparation time: 30-40 minutes
Cooking time: 40-45 minutes
Oven: 180°C, 350°F, Gas Mark 4

1. If using fresh cranberries, place them in a pan with sufficient water to cover. Bring to the boil and simmer until the cranberries all 'pop'. Continue cooking until nearly all the liquid has evaporated, then add the sugar and cook for another few minutes, until the mixture is quite stiff.
2. If using cooking apples, par-cook for 4-5 minutes in a very little water.
3. Place the apples in a bowl with the cranberries, or cranberry sauce and add the lemon rind, lemon juice, hazelnuts, brown sugar, raisins, spices and salt. Stir well and leave for the flavours to blend while the pastry is made.
4. Rub the fats lightly into the flour, then bind with the egg yolk and sufficient water to give a firm dough. Knead lightly until the pastry is smooth.
5. Roll out three-quarters of the pastry and use it to line a 23 cm (9 inch) loose-bottomed fluted flan tin. Fill the flan with the apple and cranberry mixture. Roll out the rest of the dough and cut into 1 cm (½ inch) strips. Cover the top of the flan with a lattice of pastry strips.
6. Brush the lattice with egg white and sprinkle with caster sugar.
7. Place the flan tin on a baking sheet and bake in a preheated oven for 40 minutes until well browned.

BEIGNETS ET SAUCE D'ABRICOTS
Fritters with Apricot Sauce

Makes 8-10

Choux pastry made with 65 g (2½ oz) flour (page 10)
1 × 400 g (14 oz) can apricots
oil, for deep frying
2 tablespoons rum (optional)
2-3 tablespoons caster sugar

Preparation time: 15 minutes
Cooking time: 25-30 minutes

1. Make the choux pastry.
2. Liquidize the apricots with sufficient juice from the can to give a thick purée.
3. Heat a deep pan of oil to 165°C, (330°F) or until a cube of bread browns in 60 seconds.
4. Carefully place large teaspoonfuls of the pastry in the hot oil. Be sure to cook only a few at a time, as they need room in the pan to rise. Cook each batch for 10-12 minutes, turning occasionally until crisp and golden brown. Remove from the pan with a slotted spoon and drain for a few minutes on paper towels. Sprinkle with sugar, pile into a serving dish and keep hot.
5. Heat the apricot purée and add the rum if using, or more of the juice. Serve in a sauce boat.

Variations:
Other fruits can also be used for the sauce. 225-350 g (8-12 oz) raspberries, sieved and mixed with 2-3 tablespoons icing sugar, or the same amount of cooked, sweetened blackberries, puréed, are ideal. Serve at once.

Use 2 teaspoons dipped in hot oil to mould each beignet before dropping them into the pan. The choux pastry will then slide easily into the hot oil.

LEFT TO RIGHT: Tarte aux canneberges et pommes; Tarte aux pommes et amandes

TARTE AUX POMMES ET AMANDES
Apple and Almond Tart

Serves 4-6
100 g (4 oz) plain flour, sifted
1 tablespoon caster sugar
50 g (2 oz) butter or hard margarine
1 egg, beaten
Filling:
450 g (1 lb) cooking apples, peeled, cored and chopped
1-2 tablespoons caster sugar
40 g (1½ oz) flaked almonds
40 g (1½ oz) melted butter
whipping cream, to serve (optional)

Preparation time: 30 minutes, plus resting the pastry
Cooking time: 30-35 minutes
Oven: 200°C, 400°F, Gas Mark 6

1. Sift the flour and sugar together into a bowl. Rub in the butter or margarine until the mixture resembles fine breadcrumbs. Blend together with the egg. Knead lightly until smooth, then wrap in cling film or greaseproof paper and refrigerate for 30 minutes.
2. Roll out the pastry and use it to line an 18 cm (7 inch) loose-bottomed fluted flan tin. Mix the chopped apple with the sugar, adding more sugar if the apples are very sharp. Place them in the pastry case and sprinkle the top with the flaked almonds and then the melted butter.
3. Place on a baking sheet and cook in a preheated oven for 30-35 minutes, until the apples are cooked. If the top seems to be browning too quickly, cover with greaseproof paper. Serve warm, with cream.

DÉLICES AUX NOIX
Coffee and Nut Creams

Makes 8
150 g (6 oz) plain chocolate, broken into pieces
300 ml (½ pint) double cream
2-3 tablespoons Tia Maria
50 g (2 oz) walnut pieces, finely chopped
8 whole walnut halves

Preparation time: 30-40 minutes

1. Melt the chocolate in a bowl over a pan of hot water. Take care not to overheat.
2. With a teaspoon, coat the sides and base of 8 paper bun cases. Use 3-4 together for firmness. Leave in the refrigerator until set, then coat the sides again. Leave to set. [A] Peel off the paper cases.
3. Meanwhile, whip the cream until it is stiff and gradually beat in the Tia Maria. Add the chopped walnuts and spoon or pipe into the prepared cases. Decorate each with a walnut half. Keep cool.

[A] The chocolate cases can be made several days in advance. Store in the refrigerator, wrapped in cling film, and peel off the paper cases when required.

Variation:
For a more economical version, dissolve 2 teaspoons instant coffee in 3-4 teaspoons boiling water. Use instead of the Tia Maria and beat sufficient into the cream to give a good coffee flavour.

Spooning chocolate into paper cases

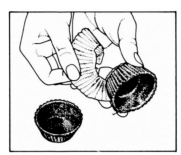
Peeling off the paper from the chocolate

SUPRÊME AU CHOCOLAT
Chocolate Supreme

Serves 8-10
175 g (6 oz) plain chocolate, broken into pieces
175 g (6 oz) madeira cake crumbs
175 g (6 oz) ground almonds
40 g (1½ oz) glacé cherries, chopped
40 g (1½ oz) mixed peel, finely chopped
grated rind of 1 orange or lemon
50 g (2 oz) unsalted butter
2 egg yolks
4 tablespoons rum or Cointreau
2-3 drops almond essence
Topping:
150 ml (¼ pint) double or whipping cream
a little grated chocolate

Preparation time: 1½ hours

This gâteau needs to be made at least 24 hours in advance.

1. Line the base of a 15 cm (6 inch) loose-bottomed cake tin with a circle of non-stick silicone paper.
2. Melt the chocolate in a bowl over a pan of hot water, taking care not to overheat it. Spread most of the chocolate over the base and sides of the tin. A dessert spoon is ideal for this. Place it in the refrigerator to set, then coat the sides again and refrigerate.
3. Mix the cake crumbs with the ground almonds, glacé cherries, mixed peel and grated rind.
4. In another bowl, beat the butter until it is soft, then beat in the egg yolks, a little at a time, and finally the rum or Cointreau. Beat in 2-3 drops almond essence. Taste, and add more if necessary. Press the mixture firmly and evenly into the prepared chocolate case and refrigerate overnight. F
5. To finish the gâteau, quickly dip the cake tin into hand hot water. Slide the gâteau out of the tin onto a plate. Refrigerate again for a few moments, then remove the base of the tin. With a sharp knife, cut off the surplus chocolate level with the filling. Smooth the sides with a round-bladed knife, if necessary.
6. Whip the remainder of the cream until it is stiff and pile it into the centre of the gâteau to cover the filling. Sprinkle a little grated chocolate over the cream. Serve well chilled.
F To freeze, wrap very carefully in cling film and store on a rack in the freezer. Thaw overnight in the refrigerator.

> To coat the cake tin with chocolate, use the same method as shown with the Délices (page 70), using a dessert spoon instead of a teaspoon. To coat the sides, hold the tin at a 45° angle and smooth round with the spoon, spreading the chocolate evenly over the surface. Allow the chocolate to harden completely before applying the second coat. The chocolate shell will come out of the tin quite easily once the tin has been dipped into hot water. Use a palette knife to release the base.

Suprème au chocolat

CREMETS D'ANGERS
Anjou Cream Hearts

Makes 8
225 g (8 oz) curd or full fat soft cheese
150 ml (¼ pint) double cream
300 ml (½ pint) soured cream
2 egg whites
225 ml (7½ fl oz) single cream (optional)
225 g (8 oz) small strawberries

Preparation time: 30 minutes

These must be made the day before they are required.

1. Line 8 small heart-shaped moulds with a single layer of muslin. If these are not available, use small cream or yogurt pots and punch a few holes in the bottom of each with a hot skewer.
2. Blend the cheese with 2-3 tablespoons double cream. Mix the remaining double and soured cream together in a bowl and whisk until they are thick and stand in soft peaks. Mix the cheese and cream well together.
3. Whisk the egg whites until stiff and carefully fold into the mixture.
4. Spoon the mixture into the prepared moulds and leave on a tray, in the refrigerator, to drain overnight. Turn out the moulds onto a serving dish and pour a little single cream over each one just before serving, if liked. Decorate with small strawberries, and serve with caster sugar.

Variation:
Instead of strawberries, serve the Cremets with fresh raspberries, or raspberry jelly. They taste delicious served with a soft fruity white wine such as Vouvray or Sancerre.

LEFT TO RIGHT: Tulipes aux fraises (page 74); Cremets d'Angers

TULIPES AUX FRAISES
Strawberry Tulips

Serves 8-10
1-2 small oranges
2 egg whites
65 g (2½ oz) caster sugar, sifted
2-3 drops vanilla essence
50 g (2 oz) plain flour, sifted
50 g (2 oz) hazelnuts, finely chopped
50 g (2 oz) butter, melted and cooled
a little icing sugar
To finish:
Strawberry sorbet
150 ml (¼ pint) whipping cream, whipped
8-10 strawberries (optional)

Preparation time: 15 minutes
Cooking time: 20-30 minutes
Oven: 200°C, 400°F, Gas Mark 6

1. Lightly grease and flour 2-3 baking sheets and grease the oranges to be used for moulding.
2. Whisk the egg whites until thick and frothy. Add the sugar and beat again until thick and white.
3. Add the vanilla essence to the melted butter.
4. Fold the flour into the mixture about a third at a time, alternating with the melted butter. Fold in the chopped nuts.
5. Put small teaspoonfuls of the mixture onto the prepared baking sheets, taking care to keep them widely spaced. Spread each one out to a thin 10 cm (4 inch) circle. Sift a little icing sugar over each one and bake in a preheated oven for 5-6 minutes until the edges are lightly coloured.
6. Lift off with a palette knife and quickly mould over an orange to form a cup. It is important to work quickly at this stage as the biscuits set very quickly when they have been removed from the oven, so it is advisable not to cook more than 3-4 at a time. Cool on a wire tray and store in an airtight tin until required. [A]
7. To serve, place a scoop of strawberry sorbet in each cup. If liked, pipe a swirl of whipped cream on the top of each and finish with a strawberry. Serve immediately.
[A] The biscuits can be made in advance and will keep up to 4 weeks in an airtight tin.

SORBET AUX FRAISES
Strawberry Sorbet

100 g (4 oz) granulated sugar
150 ml (¼ pint) water
450 g (1 lb) strawberries, puréed and sieved
3-4 tablespoons lemon juice
2 egg whites

Preparation time: 15-20 minutes

1. Dissolve the sugar in the water over a gentle heat. Add the strawberry purée with the lemon juice. Chill.
2. Pour the mixture into a plastic or china bowl and cover. Place in the freezer or the frozen food compartment of a refrigerator until it is softly frozen. This takes 2-3 hours in a china bowl and 3-4 hours in a plastic one.
3. When the mixture is ready, whisk the egg whites until they are very stiff, then whisk the sorbet until it is smooth. Fold the egg whites gently and evenly into the sorbet. Pour the sorbet into a plastic box, cover and freeze overnight.
4. Remove from the freezer and stand in the refrigerator for 10-15 minutes before using.

GLACE AU CITRON ET YAOURT
Lemon and Yogurt Ice Cream

300 ml (½ pint) plain yogurt
75 g (3 oz) caster sugar
finely grated rind of lemon
3-4 tablespoons lemon juice
To decorate (optional):
6-8 tablespoons whipping cream, stiffly whipped
3-4 thin slices of lemon, cut in half
3-4 glacé cherries, cut in half (optional)

Preparation time: 15 minutes

1. Beat the yogurt and sugar together until the sugar has dissolved. Add the lemon rind and juice. Taste and add a little more sugar if the mixture is too sharp, remembering that freezing dulls the sweetness of food.
2. Cover the bowl and place in the freezer or the frozen food compartment of the refrigerator and leave until the mixture is softly frozen. Beat the ice until it is quite smooth then place in a mould or bowl and freeze overnight until solid.
3. To serve, the ice cream can be turned out onto a serving dish and decorated with the whipped cream, sliced lemon and glacé cherries (if liked).

POIRES AU CARAMEL
Caramelized Pears

4 ripe medium pears, peeled, with the stalk left on
2-3 tablespoons lemon juice
100 g (4 oz) granulated sugar
300 ml (½ pint) water
50 g (2 oz) butter

Preparation time: 10 minutes
Cooking time: 50-60 minutes
Oven: 200°C, 400°F, Gas Mark 6

The pears are delicious served alone or they can be
served with lightly whipped cream.

1. Brush each pear with lemon juice. Place in an
ovenproof dish.
2. Dissolve the sugar in 150 ml (¼ pint) water, then
bring to the boil without stirring and boil until the
syrup becomes a light golden caramel.
3. Remove from the heat. Quickly pour on the
remaining water and stir over a gentle heat until the
caramel has dissolved.
4. Pour over the pears. Cover with a lid or aluminium foil and cook for 30-40 minutes in a preheated
oven, until the pears are soft and translucent. Turn
the pears in the syrup once or twice during the
cooking time, so that they colour evenly.
5. Carefully lift out the pears with a slotted spoon
and stand upright in a serving dish. Place the syrup
in a saucepan and boil until it becomes syrupy, then
add the butter in small pieces. Pour over the pears
and leave to cool.

LEFT TO RIGHT: Glace au citron et yaourt: Poires au caramel

CRÈME BRÛLÉE AUX FRAISES
Caramel-Topped Cream with Strawberries

175 g (6 oz) small strawberries, or large ones quartered
1-2 tablespoons Kirsch (optional)
2 egg yolks
1 dessertspoon caster sugar
300 ml (½ pint) double cream
2-3 tablespoons demerara sugar

Preparation time: 10 minutes
Cooking time: 30 minutes

1. Place the strawberries in the bottom of 4 ramekins and sprinkle with the Kirsch, if using.
2. Beat the egg yolks in a bowl with the caster sugar. Heat the cream in a pan almost to boiling point and pour onto the eggs. Mix well.
3. Place the bowl over a pan of boiling water or use a double saucepan. Do not allow the bottom of the bowl or pan to touch the water. Cook the egg mixture, stirring continuously, until it thickens. Remove from the heat and allow to cool, then pour over the strawberries and refrigerate overnight.
4. Cover the top of the custard with a thin layer of sugar and place under a preheated grill until the sugar caramelizes. Cool, then chill again before serving.

CRÈME PATISSIÈRE
Pastry Cream

300 ml (½ pint) milk
1 egg
1 egg yolk
50 g (2 oz) caster sugar
25 g (1 oz) plain flour, sifted
2-3 drops vanilla essence, or other flavouring, to taste

Preparation time: 10 minutes
Cooking time: 7-10 minutes

1. Heat the milk until it begins to steam.
2. Mix the egg and egg yolk with the caster sugar and beat until creamy, then add the flour and beat until smooth.
3. Pour on the hot milk and mix well. Return to the pan and bring to the boil over a gentle heat, stirring all the time with a wire whisk. If the mixture becomes lumpy, beat hard with a whisk until smooth. Once it has come to the boil, beat over gentle heat for another 2-3 minutes. Add the vanilla essence and use as required. [A]
[A] Crème patissière can be made the day before and stored overnight in the refrigerator. Dot the top with softened butter to prevent a skin from forming over the surface.

CRÊPES AUX ORANGES ET KIWI
Pancakes with Oranges and Kiwi Fruit

300 ml (½ pint) Crêpe batter (page 22)
2 oranges
300 ml (½ pint) Crème patissière
1 kiwi fruit, peeled and sliced
1-2 tablespoons sieved icing sugar

Preparation time: 30 minutes
Cooking time: 30-40 minutes

These sweet filled pancakes are made with the same basic mixture used for Crêpes aux fruits de mer.

1. Make 4 large or 8 small pancakes (page 22) and keep hot. [A] [F]
2. Grate the rind from one orange, and with a sharp serrated knife cut off the pith and carefully remove the segments of orange. Cut each segment into 2-3 pieces. Thinly slice the other orange.
3. Make the Crème patissière, adding the grated rind to the milk. When it is thick, add the chopped orange pieces.
4. Place some of the cream down the centre of each pancake and roll up. Arrange on a hot serving dish.
5. Just before serving, sprinkle a little icing sugar over the top. Garnish with sliced oranges and kiwi fruit.
[A] Either the batter or the panckes can be made earlier in the day.
[F] Pancakes can be frozen, sandwiched between sheets of greaseproof paper. If many are needed, defrost at room temperature. A few can be defrosted and reheated over hot water. Once they have been taken out of the freezer and separated, they defrost very quickly.

Variations:
Heat 2-3 tablespoons orange jelly marmalade and pour over the pancakes instead of the icing sugar. Flambé the pancakes, which should be placed in a fireproof dish, with Cointreau, Grand Marnier or other orange-flavoured liqueur.

TOP TO BOTTOM: Pêches gratinées aux macarons;
Crêpes aux oranges et kiwi

PÊCHES GRATINÉES AUX MACARONS
Baked Stuffed Peaches

4 firm ripe peaches, peeled, cut in half and stoned
4 stale macaroons, crushed
1 tablespoon ground almonds
2 tablespoons mixed crystallized fruits, finely chopped
1 egg yolk
150 ml (¼ pint) double or whipping cream
1 tablespoon Kirsch or rum (optional)
40 g (1½ oz) icing sugar
40 g (1½ oz) unsalted butter, melted
2 tablespoons water
To finish:
2-3 tablespoons Kirsch or rum (optional)

Preparation time: 15 minutes
Cooking time: 30-35 minutes
Oven: 190°C, 375°F, Gas Mark 5

1. With a teaspoon, scoop out a little flesh from the centre of each peach half. Chop this up and mix with the macaroons, ground almonds, crystallized fruits, egg yolk, 1 tablespoon cream and 1 tablespoon Kirsch or rum if using. Stuff the peach halves with this mixture and place in a buttered fireproof dish.
2. Sprinkle the icing sugar over the top of each and brush the outsides with the melted butter. Sprinkle the rest of the butter over the top of the peaches.
3. Add 2 tablespoons water to the dish and cook in a preheated oven for about 25-30 minutes, until the peaches are cooked and the centres brown.
4. Beat the remaining cream until it stands in soft peaks and place in a serving dish.
5. When the peaches are cooked arrange them in a fireproof serving dish, warm the Kirsch or rum, if using, pour over the peaches and ignite. Serve immediately, with the whipped cream, if liked.

TARTE AUX PRUNEAUX
Prune Tart

Serves 6-8
150 g (5 oz) plain flour
2 egg yolks
50 g (2 oz) caster sugar
75 g (3 oz) butter
350 g (12 oz) medium prunes, soaked overnight
300 ml (½ pint) Crème patissière (page 76)
2-3 tablespoons rum (optional)
50-75 g (2-3 oz) blanched almonds
3-4 tablespoons redcurrant jelly

Preparation time: 45 minutes, plus resting the pastry
Cooking time: 25 minutes
Oven: 190°C, 375°F, Gas Mark 5

1. Sift the flour into a bowl, make a well in the centre and add the egg yolks, caster sugar and butter. With the fingers of one hand blend the egg yolks with the sugar and butter and gradually mix in the flour with both hands until it is all incorporated and the mixture has a crumbly appearance. Continue blending until a soft ball of dough is formed. Wrap the dough in cling film or greaseproof paper and allow to rest in the refrigerator for 20-30 minutes or until it becomes quite firm.
2. Roll out the pastry and use to line a 21.5 cm (8½ inch) fluted flan tin. Cover the inside with grease-proof paper and fill with baking beans. Bake in a preheated oven for 20 minutes, then remove the baking beans and greaseproof paper and return to the oven for a further 5 minutes to dry out. Cool on a wire tray.
3. Put the prunes and the water in which they have been soaking into a pan with a lid and simmer gently for 10-15 minutes until they are just tender. Take care not to overcook.
4. Make the Crème patissière and add the rum, if using. Pour into a bowl and sprinkle the top with a little caster sugar to prevent a skin forming.
5. When the prunes are cooked, drain and allow to cool, then make a slit in the side of each and remove the stone. Place a blanched almond in each prune so that the edge shows through each slit.
6. Spread the Crème patissière inside the cold flan case. Arrange rings of the prunes on top with the almonds showing. Heat the redcurrant jelly in a pan and beat with the whisk until it is smooth. Bring to the boil and brush over the top of the flan until completely coated with the glaze. Chill and serve cold.

GÂTEAU BASQUE
Basque Cherry Gâteau

Serves 5-6
225 g (8 oz) butter
400 g (14 oz) plain flour
225 g (8 oz) caster sugar
3 egg yolks
1 egg white
1 tablespoon rum
450 g (1 lb) black cherry jam
1 egg yolk, beaten
1-2 tablespoons milk

Preparation time: 20 minutes, plus chilling
Cooking time: 35 minutes
Oven: 180°C, 350°F, Gas Mark 4

The pastry, which is a feature of this type of French gâteau, resembles a moist scone mixture. When it is baked, it is crisp and golden brown on the outside, and has a cake-like texture on the inside. It is important to chill the pastry well before rolling it out.

1. To make this pastry successfully, the butter must be soft, but not runny or oily: take it out of the refrigerator 1-2 hours in advance. Place the butter in a bowl and beat with a wooden spoon until soft. Sift the flour and sugar onto the butter, make a well in the centre and add the egg yolks, the egg white and the rum. Mix well together to form a dough, then knead lightly until smooth. Wrap in cling film or greaseproof paper and put in the refrigerator for 20-30 minutes until it is firm.
2. Grease a 23 cm (9 inch) flan ring and baking sheet. Roll out two-thirds of the pastry into a circle just large enough to line the flan ring. The pastry should be 1 cm (½ inch) thick. Avoid over-handling the pastry.
3. Brush the edge with a little beaten egg yolk and fill the centre with the cherry jam. Roll out the rest of the pastry and cover the top of the flan. Seal well and trim off any surplus pastry.
4. Score a chevron or spiral design with a fork on top of the flan. Mix the beaten yolk with a little milk and brush over the top. Bake in a preheated oven for 35 minutes. Remove the flan ring from the flan and leave to cool on the baking tray until it is firm enough to move, then cool on a wire tray. F
F Thaw overnight in the refrigerator.

TOP TO BOTTOM: Gâteau Basque; Tarte aux pruneaux

INDEX